TOP **10**
ITALIAN LAKES

LUCY RATCLIFFE

Left **View from Lake Como ferry** Right **Entrance of the Rocca Scaligera, Sirmione**

LONDON, NEW YORK,
MELBOURNE, MUNICH AND DELHI
www.dk.com

Reproduced by Colourscan, Singapore
Printed and bound in China by South China
Printing Co. Ltd.

First published in Great Britain in 2011
by Dorling Kindersley Limited,
80 Strand, London WC2R 0RL
A Penguin Company

**Copyright 2011 © Dorling
Kindersley Limited, London**

A CIP catalogue record is available from the
British Library

ISBN 9781 4053 5872 9

Within each Top 10 list in this book, no
hierarchy of quality or popularity is implied.
All 10 are, in the editor's opinion, of roughly
equal merit.

MIX
Paper from
responsible sources
FSC™ C018179
www.fsc.org

Contents

The Italian Lakes' Top 10

The Italian Lakes'
Highlights   6

Isola Bella   8

Northern Lake Maggiore   10

Orta San Giulio   12

Como   14

Milan   16

Verona   20

Centro Lago and
its Villages   22

Bergamo   24

Lake Idro and
the Valvestino   26

Sirmione and Southern
Lake Garda   28

Moments in History   32

Walks   34

Festivals   36

Outdoor Sports   38

Cycling Routes   40

The information in this DK Eyewitness Top 10 Travel Guide is checked regularly.
Every effort has been made to ensure that this book is as up-to-date as possible at the time of
going to press. Some details, however, such as telephone numbers, opening hours, prices,
gallery hanging arrangements and travel information are liable to change. The publishers
cannot accept responsibility for any consequences arising from the use of this book, nor for
any material on third party websites, and cannot guarantee that any website address in this
book will be a suitable source of travel information. We value the views and suggestions of
our readers very highly. Please write to: Publisher, DK Eyewitness Travel Guides, Dorling
Kindersley, 80 Strand, London WC2R 0RL, or email travelguides@uk.dk.com

Left **Rocca Borromeo interiors** Centre **Windsurfers on Lake Como** Right **Le Biciclette restaurant**

Culinary Specialities 42

Works of Art 44

Swimming Spots 46

Gardens 48

Children's Attractions 50

Elegant Bars & Cafés 52

Shopping 54

Great Journeys 56

Around Town

Lake Maggiore and Around 60

Lake Como and Around 70

Bergamo, Brescia and Lake Iseo 76

Lake Garda and Around 84

Milan and Southern Lombardy 92

Streetsmart

Planning Your Trip 102

Getting To and Around the Italian Lakes 103

Useful Information 104

Special Interest Holidays 105

Banking and Communications 106

Security and Health 107

Things to Avoid 108

Budget Tips 109

Dining Tips 110

Accommodation Tips 111

Places to Stay 112

General Index 118

Italian Lakes Town Index 128

Left **Façade of the Duomo, Milan** Right **Botanical garden at Villa Taranto, Lake Maggiore**

THE ITALIAN
LAKES'
TOP 10

The Italian Lakes'
Highlights 6–7

Isola Bella 8–9

Northern Lake
Maggiore 10–11

Orta San Giulio
12–13

Como 14–15

Milan 16–19

Verona 20–21

Centro Lago and its
Villages 22–23

Bergamo 24–25

Lake Idro and the
Valvestino 26–27

Sirmione and Southern
Lake Garda 28–29

ITALIAN LAKES' TOP 10

🔟 The Italian Lakes' Highlights

The spectacular natural beauty of the Italian Lakes region, sheltering under the Alps at the top of Italy, is matched by its historical legacy. Attractive lake villages, laidback resorts and pretty towns offer a variety of fine art, architecture and cuisine, as well as unlimited opportunities for walking, cycling and watersports activities. The climate is special too, with the larger lakes acting as solar batteries producing a temperate climate.

Isola Bella
The sumptuous rooms of the palace of Isola Bella on Lake Maggiore only begin to prepare you for the extravagant terraced gardens and their grottoes *(see pp8–9)*.

Northern Lake Maggiore
Italy melts into Switzerland at the northern end of Lake Maggiore and the Alps loom larger. Stunning displays of flora flourish in the lake's peculiar micro-climate in the small, attractive resorts dotted around here *(see pp10–11)*.

Orta San Giulio
Lake Orta's honey-coloured village, Orta San Giulio, is nestled between the quiet woods of its Sacro Monte, or Holy Mountain, and the lake with Isola San Giulio opposite *(see pp12–13)*.

Como
Wrapped around a bay at the southern end of Lake Como, the silk-producing town of Como is a historical place with a grand cathedral and cobbled streets within a medieval wall *(see pp14–15)*.

Preceding pages **Isola Bella, Lake Maggiore**

Verona
Just east of Lake Garda, romantic Verona is the perfect blend of ancient streets, historical buildings and fine food and wine *(see pp20–21)*.

Milan
Famous as the home of fashion and design, Milan also boasts ancient churches, a magnificent Gothic cathedral and a host of museums *(see pp16–17)*.

Centro Lago and its Villages
At the centre of Lake Como – the Centro Lago – where the three branches of the lake meet, stands Bellagio, with its pretty village centre of stepped streets *(see pp22–3)*.

LOMBARDIA

VENETO

20 ⌐ miles ¬ 0 ⌐ km ¬ 20

Bergamo
Venetian walls surround Bergamo's upper town, while orchards and vineyards tumble down the hillside to the 19th-century avenues of the lower town *(see pp24–5)*.

Lake Idro and the Valvestino
The villages and hamlets in this forgotten corner of Lombardy sandwiched between Lake Garda and Lake Iseo shelter clean waters, pristine countryside and a pace of life rarely found in 21st-century Europe *(see pp26–7)*.

Sirmione and Southern Lake Garda
The very popular resort of Sirmione with its Roman ruins and remarkably intact medieval castle juts out into the sapphire waters of Southern Lake Garda. Nearby, there is a host of attractive lakeside villages that boast ancient centres, Grand Hotels and excellent beaches *(see pp28–9)*.

🔟 Isola Bella

Once home to a fishing village, this craggy little island on Lake Maggiore was acquired in 1632 by the aristocratic Borromeo family and named for Carlo III's wife, Isabella (the name being contracted to Isola Bella). The island was transformed into a vast garden-and-palace complex by architects Giovanni Angelo Crivelli and Andrea Biffi, who created the dizzying series of chambers that comprise the palace, and sculpted the garden into high terraces, erupting with cypress and citrus trees. It is hard not to be seduced by the artful planting, exuberant statuary and the white peacocks that stalk the gardens.

Intricately decorated interior of a grotto

✪ Try to arrive early when the palace opens: this is the best way to avoid crowds, which can be overwhelming in July and August.

🍴 The palace café, located behind the Teatro Massimo, is a better bet for a simple lunch than the run-of-the-mill stalls clustered by the waterfront.

• Map J3
• Ferry from Baveno, Stresa or Pallanza
• Open daily Apr–Oct 9am–5:30pm
• Adm €12
• www. borromeoturismo.it

Top 10 Features

1. Stanza dello Zuccarelli
2. Sala di Napoleone
3. Borromeo Chapel
4. Galleria degli Arazzi
5. Grottoes
6. Teatro Massimo
7. Sala da Ballo
8. Giardino d'Amore
9. Sala delle Medaglie
10. Atrio di Diana

1 Stanza dello Zuccarelli

Named after the Rococo painter Francesco Zuccarelli, the walls of this stanza are adorned with his picturesque scenes *(above)* of rich and frolicsome 18th-century maidens in idealized sylvan landscapes.

2 Sala di Napoleone

Salmon pink walls decorated with paintings, ornate stucco work, rich furnishings and a tall brocade bed are the highlights of this elegant and sumptuous room

3 Borromeo Chapel

Built in the 1840s in high Gothic style rather than in the elaborate Baroque mode that characterizes the rest of the palace, this private chapel is the lofty tomb of Vitaliano and Giovanni Borromeo, carved in Carrara marble.

(right) in which Napoleon and his wife Josephine slept when they stayed on the island in 1797.

Galleria degli Arazzi
This long gallery is hung with wonderfully intricate 16th-century Flemish tapestries. These vivid works of art *(above)* feature unicorns, lions and scarlet birds in fantastical woodland settings.

Grottoes
A retreat for the hot summer months, this is an extraordinary series of cave-like chambers down at water level. Every inch of the grottoes' surface is encrusted with coloured stones. There is the odd marble statue too, including a recumbent naked woman.

Teatro Massimo
The Teatro Massimo is the dramatic high point of the island's gardens, with tiers of cherubs, Greek gods and obelisks. There are sweeping views of the lake from the upper terrace *(above)*.

Sala da Ballo
Adorned with classical pillars and embracing statues, the large and elegant marble ballroom *(above)* is the dramatic centrepiece of the palace chambers.

Giardino d'Amore
These Italianate gardens *(main image)* sit below the Teatro Massimo, and look rather restrained in comparison to its grandeur. The twirling symmetrical topiary of the garden is punctuated with bright rose bushes.

Sala delle Medaglie
Named for the ten gilded wooden medallions placed above the doors, this was the banqueting chamber *(above)* of the palace. You can't miss the magnificent 18th-century Murano crystal chandelier, the highlight of the room.

Atrio di Diana
A pretty alcove *(above)*, lush with ferns and mosses. A wistful statue of Diana the huntress at its centre is the romantic entry point to the gardens.

The Stresa Music Festival

Founded in 1961, this festival of classical music (Aug–mid-Sep) has spread well beyond the boundaries of Stresa itself, including Isola Bella: a magical venue for an open-air concert. Check www.stresafestival.eu for details, and book tickets well in advance. Other likely locations include Santa Caterina *(see p62)*, and the Rocca Borromeo, as well as various other villas and churches.

Northern Lake Maggiore

Lake Maggiore (also called Verbano), narrows at its northern tip with steep mountain ranges pushing in on the resorts and lakeside towns. Italy merges into Switzerland for the final loop of the lake where the roads improve dramatically. Sleepy attractive Italian villages dot the area while further ahead there are the well established holiday resorts in Swiss towns. The climate around the lake is ideal for sailing and windsurfing and also encourages banks of camellias, rhododendrons and palm trees that line the shores.

Statue, Isole di Brissago

🚗 Motorists will find that petrol is cheaper in Switzerland. There are few petrol stations near the border on the Italian side.

• Lake Maggiore Express: Map K2; One-day pass €30; tickets available from ferry companies, train stations, tourist offices and travel agents around the lake
• Cannobio: Via A Giovanola; Map B2
• Scuola Windsurf La Darsena: Via Provinciale, Pino; Map B2; 339 292927; Open May–Sep
• Cannero Riviera: Piazza degli Alpini; Map K2
• Ascona: Via Papio; Map L1
• Luino: Via Piero Chiara; Map K3
• Locarno: Via B Luini 3; Map B1
• Isole di Brissago: Map K2; ferry from Porto Ronco, Locarno & Ascona; Open Mar–Oct 9am–6pm; CHF 8

Top 10 Features

1. Lake Maggiore Express
2. Sunday Market, Cannobio
3. Windsurfing, Pino
4. Cannero Riviera
5. Ascona
6. Wednesday Market, Luino
7. Locarno
8. Orrido di Sant'Anna, Cannobio
9. Isole di Brissago
10. Santuario della Pietà, Cannobio

1 Lake Maggiore Express

A round-trip that combines a boat on Lake Maggiore *(main image)*, the spectacular Centovalli Railway and a fast train back to the lakeshore. This is a good value way to explore the mountains and take in the beautiful scenery around the lake.

2 Sunday Market, Cannobio

One of the lake's most attractive villages is taken over every Sunday morning by a market *(above)* along the waterfront. Stalls offer everything from fresh local produce to leather goods, cheap shoes and clothing. There is also a wide selection of food available at the market.

3 Windsurfing, Pino

Just short of the border with Switzerland, on the eastern shore of Maggiore, Pino offers many windsurfing *(below)* and kitesurfing opportunities. There are courses available for all levels, plus board hire.

4 Cannero Riviera
In a corner of the western shore, this pretty resort village *(above)* of cobbled lanes boasts a blue-flag beach and a boating harbour facing two tiny islands.

5 Ascona
Galleries and craft shops crowd the cobbled streets that lead back from picturesque Piazza Motta at the lakefront in this Swiss town. Ascona is a big attraction for northern Europeans, especially artists.

6 Wednesday Market, Luino
Bus- and ferry-loads of visitors head for the weekly market *(left)* at Luino, on the eastern shore of the lake. The stalls here offer everything, often including the kitchen sink.

7 Locarno
The Swiss resort of Locarno *(right)* has been welcoming visitors since Roman times. Its highlights include the 14th-century Castello Visconteo and artworks in the 17th-century Casa Rusca.

8 Orrido di Sant'Anna, Cannobio
At the start of Val Cannobino, the Orrido di Sant'Anna is a spectacular gorge marked by a medieval church and a restaurant. The pebbly river beach makes an ideal picnic spot.

10 Santuario della Pietà, Cannobio
Located on the waterfront, the lovely 16th-century Santuario della Pietà *(above)* was built on the orders of Cardinal Carlo Borromeo when the village was spared the worst of a plague that decimated the local population.

9 Isole di Brissago
The tiny islands of Sant'Apollinare and San Pancrazio that lie just offshore in Switzerland comprise the Isole di Brissago. San Pancrazio, the larger island, has a luxuriant botanical garden.

A Farewell to Arms

Ernest Hemmingway's World War I novel *A Farewell to Arms* is set on the Italian Front, in Milan and on Lake Maggiore. American ambulance driver Frederic Henry drinks martinis in Stresa before being reunited with British nurse Catherine Barkley. To escape the Italian authorities they row through the night to cross the border into Switzerland.

Remember to carry your passport with you if crossing over the border between Italy and Switzerland.

10 Orta San Giulio

Lake Orta (also known as Cusio), the westernmost of the Italian lakes, lies entirely within the region of Piemonte, and is characterized by soft hills and steep wooded slopes of chestnut trees flanking its sides. The highlight is the delightful lakeside village of Orta San Giulio – a string of cobbled lanes and attractive Liberty villas. Above the village is the striking Sacro Monte, an atmospheric sanctuary with spectacular views over the waters, and just offshore, the tiny island of Isola San Giulio offers a retreat from the modern world.

Cheese at Orta's Wednesday market

⦿ Some 3 km (2 miles) out of Orta San Giulio is the Orta-Miasino station – a stop on the small Novara-Domodossola branch line.

⊜ The *gastronomia* on the central Piazza Motta will make up your favourite *panino* to take away.

• Map J4
• Tourist office: Orta San Giulio: Via Panoramica; 0322 905 163; Closed Mon & Tue; Via Bossi 11; 0322 90155; Closed Tue
• Isola San Giulio: Boats from Piazza Motta leave every 30 mins from 9am–6:30pm • Sacro Monte di San Francesco: 0322 911 960; Open winter: 9am–4:30pm, summer: 9:30am –6:30pm • Il Trenino: Via Panoramica; Open 1 Mar–31 Oct: 9am–7pm, after 4pm on Wed; Nov–Feb: Sun only • Basilica di San Giulio: Open Oct–Mar: 9:30am–5:45pm; Apr–Sep: 9:30am–7pm
• Leon d'Oro: Piazza Motta 42; 0322 91 1991

Top 10 Features

1. Market
2. Rowing on the Lake
3. Sacro Monte di San Francesco
4. Isola San Giulio
5. Via Olina
6. Palazzo della Comunità
7. Il Trenino
8. Basilica di San Giulio
9. Piazza Motta
10. Leon d'Oro

Market

Since 1228, Orta's Wednesday market has taken over the main waterside square of Piazza Motta, offering a host of fresh local produce – vegetables, fruit, salami, cheese and meat.

Rowing on the Lake

Lake Orta is perfectly scenic and great for a spot of rowing *(above)*. Boatmen on Piazza Motta rent out rowing boats by the hour.

Sacro Monte di San Francesco

Winding through the nature reserve above town is the Sacro Monte (Holy Mountain) path, lined with 20 chapels *(right)* with 17th–18th-century terracotta works from the life of Saint Francis of Assisi.

Isola San Giulio

The quiet wooded island of San Giulio *(main image)* is located west of Orta San Giulio. Reached by a shuttle boat service from Piazza Motta, it is home to a community of nuns. The 19th-century Benedictine seminary and graceful bell tower dominate the skyline while the basilica, a convent, and a few villas occupy the other buildings.

For more on Lake Orta, visit www.orta.net

Via Olina

5 Narrow cobbled Via Olina *(left)* is Orta's main thoroughfare, named after one of the Renaissance *palazzi* that line the street. A pleasant mix of eclectic boutiques and delicatessens offer souvenirs to take home.

Palazzo della Comunità

6 Built in 1582, the lovely Palazzo Motta in the main square is raised up on porticoes and reached by an external staircase. The court and council room is decorated by the Baroque fresco, *Madonna and Francesco and Giulio.*

Il Trenino

7 This little motorized train *(below)* trundles through the streets taking the puff out of Orta's steep gradients. A trip between the hilltop tourist office and Piazza Motta is covered in 30 minutes.

Basilica di San Giulio

8 The island-church was founded in the first century AD, although the current building is from the 10th century with Baroque touch-ups. Frescoes depicting the saints' lives line the walls inside the church. Do not miss the 12th-century black marble pulpit covered with allegorical carvings of good versus evil.

Piazza Motta

9 The village alleyways wind around the heart of Orta – the Piazza Motta *(below)* – a broad piazza dotted with cafés and lakeside benches. A lovely spot to watch the world go by.

Saint Julius (San Giulio)

According to legend, Julius arrived in Orta in 390 AD from his native Greece, escaping persecution as a Christian. At the time, the island was guarded by serpents and dragons and no one was willing to row him to it. Julius used his cape as a sail and single-handedly rid the island of the beasts and built the church that also houses his remains.

Leon d'Oro

10 In a region of idyllic locations, it still does not get much better than at the Leon d'Oro. The restaurant is part of a family-run hotel with few pretensions and boasts a lovely terrace over the water.

TOP 10 Como

Nestled at the foot of the Alps, the affluent little lakeside town of Como has been an important place commercially and politically since pre-Roman times. After invading armies stopped vying for its attention in the late 19th century, Como became a wealthy backwater, combining textile manufacturing with its role as staging post for the many tourists here to enjoy the romantic delights of Lake Como. The partly walled old town is a pleasant maze of cobbled pedestrianized streets leading down to the palm-lined waterfront promenade.

Villa Geno, Como

🚢 A ferry with a picture of a knife and fork on the timetable means that there is a restaurant on board.

• Map M4
• Como: Piazza Cavour 17; Open daily 9am–1pm & 2:30–6pm; 031 269712
• The Duomo: Piazza del Duomo; Open daily 7am–noon, 3–7pm
• The Funicular: Piazza de Gasperi; Open daily 6am–10:30pm, Jun–mid-Sep closes 12pm; return €4.50
• Villa Olmo: Via Cantoni; 031 576 169 (garden), Open daily 8/9am–7/11pm
• Museo Civico: Piazza Medaglie d'Oro 3; Open Tue–Sat 9:30am–12:30pm & 2–5pm, Sun 10am–1pm; ferry information at Piazza Cavour
• San Fedele: Piazza San Fedele; Open daily 8am–noon & 3–7pm
• Villa Geno: Viale Geno 12; open daily 10am–6/9pm
• Sant'Abbondio: Via Sant'Abbondio Open daily winter: 8am–4:30pm, summer: 8am–6pm

Top 10 Features

1. The Duomo
2. The Funicular
3. Villa Olmo
4. Brunate
5. Museo Civico
6. Palazzo Terragni
7. Boat Trips
8. San Fedele
9. Villa Geno
10. Sant'Abbondio

The Duomo
Como's cathedral *(below)* is a harmonious mix of architectural styles. The sweeping lines of the Gothic façade blend with a Renaissance rose window and is topped with a Baroque dome.

Villa Olmo
A grand 17th-century villa on the site of an ancient elm forest, Villa Olmo has sumptuous, frescoed interiors that are used to host temporary exhibitions. The villa's formal lakefront gardens make a pleasant public park.

Brunate
Perched at the top of the funicular track, little Brunate offers wonderful views across Como and the lake, and is the starting point of many trails into the hills. Cafés and restaurants here are especially busy for Sunday lunch.

The Funicular
Como's little yellow funicular train *(below)* hauls up and down between the town's villas and gardens. The funicular station is in the northeast corner of Como, and is easily reached by foot. The steep climb takes 7 minutes to reach Brunate at the top of the hill.

Museo Civico
The quiet little Museo Civico *(above)*, with its pretty courtyard, is housed in two elegant *palazzi*. Roman artifacts, period costumes and memorabilia from the Italian Unification period are on display.

Palazzo Terragni
Designed by Italian architect Giuseppe Terragni as the local Fascist Party headquarters in the 1930s, the harmonious proportions of Palazzo Terragni are seen as the definitive example of Rationalist architecture for their light, functional beauty.

Boat Trips
Regular ferries link the villages scattered around the area up and down the lake. Hydrofoil express services and more leisurely sightseeing cruises are also available. Boat services from Como run all year round with a reduced timetable in winter.

San Fedele
Founded in 914, San Fedele *(left)* was once Como's cathedral. It has a striking octagonal apse and 14th-century frescoes as well as an ornate door decorated with portly figures and a griffin.

A Centre for Silk

Como has been Europe's most important silk centre since the 14th century. Although these days the raw fibre is imported, Como is still renowned for its top quality silk goods crafted for designer labels. Small, family-run factories dotted around the outskirts of the town specialize in the low-run, exclusive and high quality merchandise demanded by the world's leading fashion houses such as Gucci, Versace, Hermès and Chanel.

Villa Geno
A 30-minute stroll around the bay from Como centre brings you to the grounds of Villa Geno, where the splendid fountain on the waterfront is a must see.

Sant'Abbondio
Consecrated to the patron saint of Como in 1095, this attractive Romanesque church has colourful Byzantine frescoes adorning its walls *(right)*.

Remember to carry your passport if you are visiting Switzerland, 5 km (3 miles) away from Como.

☐10 Milan

Milan is the economic heart of Italy: the centre of banking, publishing and industry as well as a design and fashion capital of the world. Guarding the route from Rome to central Europe and linked to the Adriatic sea by a series of waterways, it has always been a strategic political and commercial hub. Milan was badly bombed by the Allied forces during World War II leaving a disjointed mix of architectural styles. But it is a beguiling place with a wealth of treasures hidden in its medieval lanes, 19th-century arcades and Roman ruins.

Detail of Castello Sforzesco

🕓 The café terrace in the Rinacente store (La Rinacente, Via San Raffaele 2, Duomo Metro) offers snacks within a metre of the stone tracery of the Duomo roof.

• *The Duomo: Piazza del Duomo; Map W4; Duomo Metro; Open daily 7am–7pm; Roof €5, €8 by elevator*
• *Pinacoteca di Brera: Via Brera 28; Map W2; Montenapoleone Metro; Open Tue–Sun 8:30am–7:15pm; €11* • *La Scala: Piazza della Scala; Map W3; Duomo Metro*
• *Castello Sforezesco: Piazza Castello; Map U2; Cairoli/Cadorna Metro; Open Tue–Sun 9am–5:30pm; €3*
• *Sant'Ambrogio: Piazza Sant'Ambrogio 15; Map U4; Open daily*
• *Cenacolo Vinciano (The Last Supper): Piazza Santa Maria delle Grazie; Map T3; Metro Cadorna; 02 92 800 360; Open Tue–Sun 8:15am–6:45pm; €6:50 & €1:50 booking fee*

Top 10 Features

1. The Duomo
2. Pinacoteca di Brera
3. La Scala
4. Parco Sempione
5. Quadrilatero d'Oro
6. Galleria Vittorio Emanuele II
7. Castello Sforzesco
8. Navigli District
9. Sant'Ambrogio
10. The Last Supper

The Duomo
The third largest church in Europe, Milan's Gothic Duomo *(below)* took almost 430 years to complete. It soars up out of the central Piazza del Duomo, a confection of stone spires and statues. Clamber over the roof and enjoy the stunning views across the city.

Pinacoteca di Brera
Opened in 1809 by Napoleon as a public museum, this is the most important collection of North Italian art in the world. The Renaissance highlights include masterpieces by Raphael and Mantegna.

La Scala
The world-famous opera house opened its opulent interior to the public in 1778. Information on tickets is available from the website.

Parco Sempione
The castle's old hunting grounds *(below)* are Milan's largest extent of green. Lawns, cafés, a design museum, a children's playground and a library keep it bustling.

➥ *Avoid sightseeing on a Monday when most galleries and museums are closed.*

5 Quadrilatero d'Oro

The sleek displays *(above)* in the windows of top fashion labels are a feast for the eyes. Prices may be prohibitive but every style and taste is catered for.

6 Galleria Vittorio Emanuele II

This smart shopping arcade *(left)* opened in 1865, linking the cathedral square with the opera house. The mosaics under the glass dome celebrate the Unification of Italy.

7 Castello Sforzesco

The rambling castle complex was begun in 1368 by the rulers of Milan, the Visconti, and continued by their successors, the Sforza. Converted into a museum and gallery a century ago, its highlight is Michelangelo's unfinished sculpture, *Rondanini Pietà*.

8 Navigli District

A buzzing restaurant and bar scene has grown up around two of Milan's remaining canals *(right)*. There is a bric-a-brac market here on the last Sunday of the month.

9 Sant'Ambrogio

Founded in the 4th century by Milan's patron saint, St Ambrose, this is the city's most beautiful church. The capitals of the columns in the colonnaded atrium are decorated with horses, dragons and other beasts.

10 The Last Supper

One of the world's greatest works of art, Leonardo da Vinci's *The Last Supper (above)* was painted on a refectory wall at the Santa Maria delle Grazie monastery.

Milan's Canals

Until the beginning of the 20th century many of Milan's main thoroughfares were canals. Originally developed for defence and goods transport, the canals were eventually built over to install the speedier tram network. From the first intervention in the 11th century, the network was gradually added to until the city was linked by waterway with Switzerland and the lakes to the north and to the south, to the River Po and therefore to the Adriatic sea.

Left **Relief, bronze door** Centre **View of the roof, Duomo** Right **Statue of *St Bartholomew Flayed***

TOP 10 The Duomo

1 St Bartholomew Flayed

One of the cathedral's strangest statues is the oddly beguiling and gruesome carving of *St Bartholomew Flayed* by Marco d'Agrate (1562). The saint stands calmly with his skin flung rather jauntily over his shoulder and has fascinatingly accurate knees and toenails hanging lifelessly.

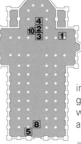

Duomo floorplan

2 Nail from the Cross

A red light on a crucifix in the ceiling marks the cathedral's most prized possession – a nail from Christ's Cross. On 14 September, a complicated system of pulleys lowers the nail down to be paraded by the Bishop of Milan.

Panel of the Five Part Ivory Diptych, Treasury

3 Scurolo di San Carlo

The bejewelled remains of San Carlo Borromeo, the city's 16th-century cardinal and champion of the poor, are laid out in the crypt. He lies in a glass coffin clothed and with a mask, gloves and a golden crown.

4 Battistero Paleocristiano

A narrow staircase leads down to the site discovered during work on the metro in the 1950s. There are the remains of Roman baths, and a 4th-century basilica, as well as the baptistery where Saint Ambrose baptized Saint Augustine in 387 AD.

5 The Façade

In 1813, the opulent façade of the Duomo was finally completed on orders from Napoleon, who was to be crowned King of Italy inside the Duomo. The soaring Neo-Gothic frontage is punctuated with a riot of colourful stained glass windows and five solid doors with bronze reliefs dating back to the 20th century.

6 Treasury

Beside the crypt under the altar, the treasury holds a fine and extensive collection of embroidered vestments, intricate 4th-century goldwork and some very early ivory carvings dating from the 10th century.

Visitors are not admitted to the cathedral with bare shoulders, shorts or above-the-knee skirts.

Top 10 Duomo Facts

1. The second largest cathedral in the world, after Seville's in Spain.
2. 2,244 statues outside, mainly of saints but including one of Napoleon.
3. 11,700 sqm internal area
4. 135 spires
5. 96 gargoyles
6. 1,100 statues inside
7. 52 columns along the central nave (one for each week of the year)
8. 158-m (518-ft) long
9. 93-m (305-ft) wide at the widest point
10. 108-m (364-ft) high

The Construction

Milan's Duomo is a massive construction worked on over four centuries by the best craftsmen and architects of their day. Surprisingly the church was completed in a more or less homogenous style – Italy's only Gothic cathedral. The first stone was laid in 1386 by the Duke of Milan, Gian Galeazzo Visconti, as an offering for an heir. The medieval management company founded to oversee the project, the Venerada Fabbrica del Duomo, is responsible for the cathedral to this day. Canals were constructed to transport building materials, including marble from quarries on Lake Maggiore. The high altar was consecrated in 1418 by Pope Martin V but the façade was not completed until 1813 when Napoleon demanded it be ready for his coronation.

Detail of the Duomo

Façade of the Duomo

Roof Terraces
One of the highlights of any visit to Milan is a wander amid the soaring white pinnacles and statues on the cathedral's marble terraces. Take the lift, or walk up the steps; follow the signs for the roof *(Salita alle terrazze)*. On a clear day, there are fantastic views over the rooftops of Milan to the Alps.

The Sundial
Just inside the main entrance is a sundial lined with zodiac signs. When installed in 1786, a ray of sunlight marked noon but it is no longer accurate because of changes in the Earth's rotation.

La Madonnina
The Madonnina, or Little Madonna, is the gilded statue perched right on the very top of the cathedral, and stands 108-m (354-ft) above ground. The original statue was placed here in 1774, but was replaced in the 1960s.

Via Dolorosa
The most unusual exhibit is also the Duomo's newest. Tucked away beside the treasury is the controversial video installation by British artist Mark Wallinger. The screen shows Zeffirelli's *Jesus of Nazareth* with 90 per cent of the image blacked out and no sound.

Little Madonna

TOP 10 Verona

Some 20 km west of Lake Garda, Verona is probably best known as the setting for William Shakespeare's *Romeo and Juliet*, but it was also one of the most important Roman towns in northern Italy and flourished in its Renaissance heyday under the della Scala family for over a century. On the main communication links between central Italy and northern Europe, Verona has always been a prosperous place and the town centre, nestling in a bend of the River Adige, is a rich patchwork of buildings from different eras.

Façade of the Duomo

• Map H4
• Verona Tourist Office: Via Degli Alpini 9; Open daily 9am–7pm, closes 4pm Sun
• The Duomo: Open Mar–Oct: Mon–Sat 10am–6pm, Sun 1pm–6pm; Nov–Feb: Tue–Sat 10am–1pm & 1:30–5pm, Sun 1–5pm; €2.50 • Casa di Giulietta: Via Cappello 23; Open daily Tue–Sun 8:30am–7:30pm, Mon 1:30–7:30pm; €6
• Castelvecchio: Corso Castelvecchio 2; Same timings as Casa di Giulietta; €6
• Sant'Anastasia: Piazza Sant'Anastasia; Same timings as the Duomo; €2.50
• Torre dei Lamberti: Cortile Mercato Vecchio; Open daily Jun–Sep: 8:30am–8:30pm, closes 11pm Fri; Oct–May: daily 8:30am–7:30pm; €6
• The Arena: Piazza Brà; Same timings as Casa di Giulietta; €6
• San Fermo: Same timings as the Duomo; €2.50 • San Zeno Maggiore: Same timings as the Duomo; €2.50
• Teatro Romano: Same timings as Casa di Giulietta; €4.50

Top 10 Features

1. The Duomo
2. Casa di Giulietta
3. Castelvecchio
4. Sant'Anastasia
5. Torre dei Lamberti
6. Piazza delle Erbe
7. The Arena
8. San Fermo
9. San Zeno Maggiore
10. Teatro Romano

2 Casa di Giulietta

This 13th-century *palazzo (below)* was drawn out of anonymity when tourist officials added a balcony to meet the demands of tourists. Fondling the right breast of the statue of Juliet in the courtyard will supposedly bring you a new lover.

3 Castelvecchio

The Castelvecchio is a severe red brick fortress with swallowtail battlements which extend across the river on the fortified bridge, the Ponte Scaligero. The stronghold was commissioned in 1354 by Cangrande II and now holds a worthwhile museum of sculpture and art.

1 The Duomo

A pretty porch is centred on the partly striped façade of the Romanesque cathedral designed by the architect Sanmicheli. The Gothic interiors contain lovely frescoes.

4 Sant'Anastasia

Verona's pink-hued marble softens the lines of the interior *(below)* of this Gothic church and acts as a backdrop for Pisanello's fresco *St George Preparing to Save the Maiden* in the chapel to the right of the altar.

The Verona Card is a good value pass (€10 a day, €15 for three days). It includes public transport, entrance to museums and churches.

Torre dei Lamberti
Standing 840-m (276-ft) high in Piazza delle Erbe, this brick tower *(left)* was built between 1172 and 1463. Catch the lift or climb the 368 steps up to the top for views over the rooftops of Verona.

Piazza delle Erbe
Once the site of the Roman Forum, then a market in the Middle Ages, this bustling square *(above)* is lined by civic institutions such as the Casa dei Mercanti and the Palazzo del Comune plus various palaces, including the Della Scala Case Mazzanti.

The Arena
Every summer Verona's immense Roman amphitheatre becomes the stage for epic productions of popular operas – Verdi's *Aida* is always included. The 15,000-seat arena has a wonderful atmosphere.

San Fermo
This is two churches in one: Dominicans built a simple lower church to house the remains of saints Fermo and Rustico, and a splendid upper church for worship.

San Zeno Maggiore
Located west of the Arena is the Romanesque masterpiece of San Zeno Maggiore. The façade is centred by the "wheel-of-fortune" window and framed by a slender bell tower. Renaissance frescoes decorate the interior and Mantegna's striking *Madonna and Saints* adorns the altar.

Teatro Romano
Left abandoned for several centuries, this impressive theatre *(right)* was excavated in the 18th century and partly reconstructed. It is now a striking backdrop for many concerts and shows.

Romeo and Juliet
Shakespeare's tale of star-crossed lovers was probably based on a novel first published in 1530 by Luigi da Porto. There is little proof that the story is anything more than fiction, although Verona was famous for feuding families and records show Capuleti (Capulet) and Montecchi (Montague) families at the time of Bartolomeo I della Scala. Evidently, sights such as Romeo's house and Juliet's house and tomb are a result of local opportunism.

Note that most sights are either closed on Monday mornings or open at 1:30 pm.

21

⟿TOP 10 Centro Lago and its Villages

The point where the two branches of southern Lake Como meet is known as Centro Lago. Pretty lakeside towns, glittering water, mountain views and splendid villas with luxurious gardens conspire to steal your heart. The surrounding mountains and lake water combine to create a temperate almost Mediterranean-like climate. Three villages form a triangle across the waters with sleepy Varenna to the east, sporty Menaggio to the west and beautiful Bellagio, the most famous of all, to the south on the tip of the promontory.

Castello di Vezio, Varenna

🔵 **La Punta (19, Punta Spartivento, Bellagio) is a panoramic spot for a drink or meal.**

- Map N3
- Villa Serbelloni: Open daily (closed from Easter to the beginning of Nov & closed on Mon); € 8:50 • Villa Carlotta: Open daily 13 Mar–28 Mar & 18 Oct–14 Nov: 10am–4pm, 29 Mar–17 Oct: 9am– 6pm; €8.50
- Varenna: Via IV Novembre 7; Map N2; Open May–Sep: Mon– Sun 10:30am–4pm (closed Tue); 0340 879 046
- Castello di Vezio: Frazione Vezio, Perledo; Map N2; Open Mar–Oct: Mon–Fri 10am–6pm, Sat–Sun 10am–7pm (closed Jan & Feb); €4
- Villa del Balbianello: Via Comoedia; Open Mar 15–Nov 15: 10am–6pm (closed Mon & Wed); Gardens – €11 (guided tours villas and gardens)
- Menaggio: Piazza Garibaldi 3; Open Mon– Sat 9am–noon & 3–6pm

Top 10 Features

1. Villa Serbelloni, Bellagio
2. San Giacomo, Bellagio
3. Pescallo
4. Villa Carlotta, Tremezzo
5. Menaggio
6. Villa del Balbianello, Lenno
7. Castello di Vezio, Varenna
8. Shopping in Bellagio
9. Varenna
10. Monte San Prino

1 Villa Serbelloni, Bellagio

The lovely gardens at Villa Serbelloni are quieter than many, and while the terracing, grottoes and statuary equal its contemporaries, the views of the lake are unrivalled. The gardens can only be visited on a guided tour.

2 San Giacomo, Bellagio

In the square at the top of Bellagio, the church of San Giacomo is a wonderful example of local 12th-century Romanesque architecture. The interior of the church is rich with mosaics and home to a splendid 16th-century altar.

3 Pescallo

Over the eastern side of the Bellagio promontory, the tiny fishing hamlet of Pescallo *(above)* is a hidden delight. There is nothing better than sitting in the shade and enjoying the lake from the waterside café.

4 Villa Carlotta, Tremezzo

Best reached by boat to its own landing stage and then up the imposing scissored-staircase, the white Neo-Classical Villa Carlotta *(above)* boasts some of the finest gardens on the lake.

Menaggio

Located near the Swiss border, Menaggio *(above)* is the the perfect base to enjoy Lake Como as well as the nearby golf course, hiking and cycle routes.

Villa del Balbianello, Lenno

Perched on a lush wooded promontory on the western shore, the luxurious terraced gardens of Villa del Balbianello *(centre)* offer breathtaking views over neighbouring Isola Comacina and the centre of the lake.

Castello di Vezio, Varenna

A short and steep 20-minute walk up the mountain behind Varenna takes you to the ruins of this 17th-century castle with spectacular views, a pleasant café and bird-of-prey displays on weekends.

Shopping in Bellagio

Bellagio's stepped alleyways and main Via Garibaldi *(left)* offer a host of goodies from top-label clothes to jewellery and shoes. Carefully crafted local leather, wood and lacework are among the many other delights that are on offer.

Varenna

Enchanting Varenna *(right)* has villas with pretty gardens, a ruined castle and a maze of cobbled streets to explore. Its sleepy waterfront is the perfect spot to simply unwind.

Monte San Prino

Offering stunning views over Lake Como and the Alps beyond, Monte San Prino is a steep three-hour hike from Bellagio along a well-kept track. The tourist office has route maps.

Lake Ferries

By far the best way to explore Lake Como is by boat. Ferries, hydrofoils and cruises crisscross between shores ensuring connections to all destinations. Services are easy to use with information available at tourist offices, the information booths on landing stages and at www.navigazione.it. Tickets are good value and slightly cheaper if bought before boarding; day passes are also available. Sailings become less frequent during low season.

🔟 Bergamo

Nestled at the foot of the Alps, midway between lakes Como and Garda, this wealthy city has a long history. Conquerors, including Romans, French, Austrians and, most notably, the Venetians – who ruled for 300 years until the end of the 18th century – have left a mix of influences. The ancient upper town, Città Alta, is a tranquil warren of cobbled streets surrounded by impressive walls while the lower town, Città Bassa, is a patchwork of elegant 19th-century boulevards, imposing civic buildings and medieval lanes.

Detail of the town wall

- Map D3
- Bergamo Tourist Office: Piazzale Marconi, Città Bassa; Via Gombito 13, Città Alta; Open Mon–Sun 9am–12:30pm & 2–5:30pm • Santa Maria Maggiore and Cappella Colleoni: Piazza del Duomo, Città Alta; Open daily Apr–Oct: Tue–Sun 9am–12:30pm & 2:30–6pm; Nov–Mar: Tue–Sun 9am–12:30pm & 2:30–5pm
- Teatro Sociale: Via Colleoni 4, Città Alta
- Funicular: Viale Vittorio Emanuele II, Città Bassa, Piazza Mercato delle Scarpe, Città Alta; Open daily; €2.50 or 3-day ticket €5
- The Rocca, Museum: Via Rocca, Città Alta; Open Oct–May: Tue–Sun 9:30am–1pm, 2–5:30pm; Jun–Sep: Tue–Fri 9:30am–1pm, 2–5:30pm; Sat 9:30am–7pm; €3
- GAMEC: Via San Tomaso 53, Città Bassa; Open Tue–Sun 10am–1pm, 3–7pm • Museo Donizettiano: Via Arena 9, Città Alta; Open Jun–Sep: Tue–Sun 9:30am–1pm & 2–5:30pm; Oct–May: Tue–Fri 9:30am–1pm, Sat & Sun 9:30am–1pm & 2–5:30pm

Top 10 Features

1. Piazza Vecchia
2. Santa Maria Maggiore and Cappella Colleoni
3. Shopping
4. Palazzo della Ragione
5. Funicular
6. Teatro Sociale
7. The Rocca
8. Galleria d'Arte Moderna e Contemporanea (GAMEC)
9. The Walls
10. Museo Donizettiano

Piazza Vecchia ①
Guarded by the 52-m (170-ft) high bell tower, this square in the heart of the upper town is lined with restaurants, with a library at one end facing the impressive Palazzo della Ragione.

Santa Maria Maggiore and Cappella Colleoni ②
The fabulously over-the-top Baroque interiors of the church are a taster for the extravagant funerary chapel next door. The Renaissance excess of coloured marble *(above)* holds the tombs of a Venetian mercenary and his 15-year-old daughter.

Shopping ③
Pedestrianised Via XX Settembre in the lower town is the best place to head for clothes and shoe stores. The upper town also has a good selection of boutiques *(below)* and gourmet delicatessens, although prices are not cheap.

Many shops in Città Alta are closed on Sunday and Monday mornings and many also close for lunch from 1–3pm.

Bergamo

Palazzo della Ragione
The elegant medieval arcaded building *(above)* dominating Piazza Vecchia dates back to the 12th century. The old courthouse and council room is topped with a bas-relief of the symbol of Venice, St Mark's lion.

Funicular
Trundling up the hill in a little two-car funicular railway *(below)* through the ornate gardens of the city's splendid villas is the perfect way to arrive in Città Alta.

Teatro Sociale
Tucked away behind an often-closed door, this impressive three-tiered wooden theatre dating from 1807 had been unused since 1929. It has recently been over-hauled to once again host works of theatre.

The Rocca
The Scala del Condannato (Prisoner's Staircase) inside the Rocca leads to the Museum of History with a well-presented collection of photographs, weapons and medals.

GAMEC
Housed in a spacious 15th-century *palazzo*, Bergamo's contemporary art gallery has a small but permanent collection of modern art. It is best known for its excellent temporary exhibitions.

Arlecchino
According to tradition, Arlecchino – or Harlequin – the dull-witted clown in love with Colombina in Commedia del Arte shows hails from Bergamo. The impro-vised popular theatre originated in Italy in the 16th century and the acrobatic servant figure, commonly depicted wearing multi-coloured diamond-patterned tights, has always been played with the gruff drawling Bergamo accent in Italy.

The Walls
The high 16th-century walls *(right)* are dotted with imposing gateways. The wide leafy avenues tracing the fortifications offer glorious views over to the Alps.

Museo Donizettiano
Curio-lovers will be thrilled by the museum's collection of letters, music scores, instruments and the personal effects of Bergamo's famous composer of melodramatic opera, Gaetano Donizetti (1797–1848).

Bus 1 is a useful link between Bergamo airport, the train station, the lower funicular station and Colle Aperto in the upper town.

TOP 10 Lake Idro and the Valvestino

Stretching up from Gargnano on the western shore of Lake Garda, switchback roads transport you to a quieter world. The Valvestino is an isolated, mountainous area of hamlets and small cattle farms stretching from Lake Garda to Lake Idro. Communication only really began in the 1960s when hydroelectric works improved the roads and opened the countryside up to the outside world. Surrounded by wooded slopes, Lake Idro is popular for fishing, whilst the afternoon breeze makes sailing and windsurfing popular too.

Picturesque Lake Idro

🌿 Don't forget to bring sunscreen, a hat and suitable footwear in summer; the mountain breezes disguise the true strength of the sun.

🍴 Al Tempo Perduto (Via San Rocco, 46; 0365 99145; www. altempoperduto.it) in the cobbled lanes of Bagolino is a great place to try traditional, local dishes. There are simple rooms upstairs if you fancy staying.

• Idro Tourist Office: Via G.Matteotti 32, Vestone; Map Q3; 0365 83224; www.lagodidro.it • The Valvestino: Map Q3; www.rivieradeilimoni.it
• Gargnano Tourist Office: Piazzale Boldini 2, Lake Garda; Map R3; 0365 791 243; www. gargnanosulgarda.it
• Bagolino: Via S.Giorgio; Map Q2; 0365 99904; Canoe rental: Surfpoint, the beach in Vantone; 339 227 5994; Jun–mid-Sep; www. surfschuleidrosee.com

Top 10 Features

1. Idro
2. Ponte Caffero
3. Vesta
4. Lake Valvestino
5. Gargnano
6. Bagòss Carnival
7. Sentiero dei Contrabbandieri
8. Canoeing, Lake Idro
9. Hiking and Trekking
10. Bagolino

1 Idro
The main village on Lake Idro is located at the southern end and divided by the River Chiese *(main image)*. Idro is a small collection of houses, some basic shops, holiday facilities and a tourist office.

2 Ponte Caffero
This small settlement *(above)* at the northern end of Lake Idro once marked the border with Austria until 1918; now the frontier is simply from the province of Lombardy to Trento.

3 Vesta
A little hamlet on the eastern side of Lake Idro, Vesta has a few holiday houses and a gravel beach. It is the starting point for various hiking and cycling trails into the hills.

4 Lake Valvestino
A fjord-like slip of water formed by damming the River Toscolano in 1960, Lake Valvestino *(below)* is surrounded by steep wooded slopes. An idyllic area of mountains, meadows and wild flowers, it is perfect for walking and cycling.

Gargnano

This waterside village *(above)* is a delightful corner of Lake Garda, surprisingly ignored by tourist crowds. It has a string of Liberty villas and a few pretty harbours below olive and lemon groves.

Bagòss Carnival

The ancient traditions of the Bagòss carnival are still celebrated in Bagolino and Ponte Caffaro before Lent, when costumed dancers take to the streets.

Sentiero dei Contrabbandieri

The "Smugglers' Path" is a spectacular route *(above)* for experienced climbers along narrow ledges and sheer rock faces with views.

Canoeing, Lake Idro

Lake Idro's placid waters are ideal for novice canoeists. And for those who want their water a little whiter, there are nearby sections of the River Chiese here that have been used for national level canoeing championships.

Hiking and Trekking

This is a fantastic region for hiking and trekking: there are paths for all abilities, unspoiled nature and fabulous views. Gargnano and Idro tourist offices have details of walks *(see p105)* as does the website – www.lagodidro.it.

Bagòss Cheese

The people of these valleys have traditionally led the tough life of subsistence-level cattle farming. The seasons would be marked by the cows being moved from winter to summer pastures. A typical product of this region is the hard, strong tasting Bagoss cheese, made with partially skimmed cows' milk. After careful preparation by hand, the cheeses are put aside for three years to mature, during which time they are scraped, oiled and turned at regular intervals.

Bagolino

The lovely village of Bagolino *(right)* is the star turn in these parts – a jumble of medieval buildings with stone porticoes and archways, presided over by the church of San Giorgio with its slender bell tower.

🔟 Sirmione and Southern Lake Garda

The rolling hills around the southern section of Lake Garda are carpeted by olive groves and vineyards. This is the region's most popular lake, complete with ancient Roman remains, medieval villages and Venetian fortresses. The blue waters backed by mountain peaks and the warm Mediterranean climate are bewitching. Poking into the lake the tiny village of Sirmione is the main attraction here, with wonderfully located Roman ruins and its own natural spa.

Villa Romana, Desenzano

🔟 The well located restaurant at the **Grifone** *(see p114)* offers local staples.

• Map R5
• *Santa Maria Maggiore: Open daily 8:30am–7pm; Nov–Feb closes 4:30pm*
• *Grotte di Catullo: Open Nov–Feb: Tue–Sat 8:30am–4:30pm, Sun 9am–1pm; Mar–Oct: Tue–Sat 8:30am–7pm, Sun 9am–6pm*
• *Lido delle Bionde: Viale Gennari 28, Sirmione; Open May–Oct daily 8am–midnight*
• *Peschiera del Garda Tourist Office: Piazza Betteloni 15* • *Bardolino Tourist Office: Piazzale Aldo Moro 5*
• *Rocca Scaligera: Open Tue–Sun 8:30am–7pm, Nov–Feb closes 5pm*
• *San Pietro: Open daily 8:30am–7pm; Nov–Feb closes 4:30pm*
• *Lazise Tourist Office: Via F Fontana 14*
• *Desenzano Tourist Office: Via Porto Vecchio 34; Map Q5; Open Mon–Fri 9:30am –12:30pm & 3–6pm, Sat 9am– 12:30pm*
• *Villa Romana: Map Q5; Open Tue–Sun 8:30am–7pm; Nov–Feb closes 5pm*

Top 10 Features

1 Santa Maria Maggiore, Sirmione
2 The Lido delle Bionde, Sirmione
3 Peschiera del Garda
4 Grotte di Catullo, Sirmione
5 Bardolino
6 Rocca Scaligera, Sirmione
7 San Pietro in Mavino, Sirmione
8 Lazise
9 Desenzano
10 Villa Romana, Desenzano

1 Santa Maria Maggiore, Sirmione

Down a lane at the southern end of the village is the 15th-century church *(below, detail)* of Santa Maria Maggiore with an arcaded portico built using recycled Roman masonry. Inside, the church has one central nave.

4 Grotte di Catullo, Sirmione

Perched at the very tip of the Sirmione promontory, the open-air ruins of a large 1st-century AD Roman villa *(right)* stand among olive trees, lavender and rosemary bushes. A delightful spot with glorious views, although the links with the poet Catullus are unproved.

2 The Lido delle Bionde, Sirmione

On the eastern side of the peninsula, just below the Grotte, white slabs of rock lead into the clean waters of the lake. Here, the beach, or *lido*, offers the best place for a dip.

3 Peschiera del Garda

This old military town has imposing 16th-century Venetian fortifications. It is the main rail hub for the lake and close to the area's theme parks.

For details regarding ferry routes and prices for the whole lake see www.navigazionelaghi.it

5 Bardolino
This attractive village *(above)* on the south-eastern side of the lake gave its name to the local red wine that accompanies the lake-fish antipasti so well. Try a glass or two in the many *cantines*, or bistros, here.

6 Rocca Scaligera, Sirmione
The Rocca, a 13th-century moated fort *(left)*, guards the land entrance to Sirmione with turrets and swallowtail battlements. Climb up the steps to the towers and enjoy the views across the lake.

8 Lazise
Lazise's *(below)* role as an important Venetian port is borne witness by the villages' remaining walls and the porticoed customs house by the little port. These days it is quieter than many of the larger resorts.

7 San Pietro in Mavino, Sirmione
Like so many properties in Sirmione, this little Romanesque church was built reusing Roman blocks. The frescoes *(above)* inside date from the 13th to 16th centuries.

Southern Garda Wines
The southern end of Garda produces some of the lakes' better quality wines. Best known are the fruity Bardolino reds from the south-eastern corner, while the southern end produces very drinkable white Lugana, Garda Classico and Custoza vintages. Red Valpolicella and white Soaves are made near the eastern shore. The southwest corner produces a light rosé.

9 Desenzano
Lake Garda's main town, Desenzano, is on the Milan–Verona train line as well as just off the A4 motorway. The attractive town centre bustles with residents. The castle and old harbour are worth a visit.

10 Villa Romana, Desenzano
A short walk from Desenzano's harbour stands Villa Romana, the remains of a late-Roman villa, once the hub of a large agricultural estate here. Look out for the beautiful mosaic floors.

One of the best ways to explore this region is by bicycle. There are numerous hire outfits and lakeside cycle paths.

Left **Painting depicting Barbarossa and his sons** Centre **Coronation of Napoleon I** Right **Mussolini**

Moments in History

1 1st Century AD: Lake Como Flourishes
In the 1st century AD, the peace and security established by the Roman emperor Augustus and his successors enabled northern Italian communities to flourish. Large agricultural estates were established and holiday villas were built around the lakes by residents of Bergamo, Brescia and Milan.

2 313 AD: Edict of Milan
Emperor Constantine issued the Edict of Milan in 313, granting Christians freedom of worship. Milan became a centre of Christianity under its charismatic bishop, Ambrogio, who established numerous churches.

3 773 AD: Charlemagne Declared King of the Franks and Lombards
With the fall of Rome, Northern European tribes swept down and sacked the lands without leaders. The Lombards established themselves at Pavia but were defeated by the Frankish king, Charlemagne. His rule brought about stability and peace to Europe.

4 1176 AD: The Lombard League Defeats "Barbarossa"
After numerous attempts to conquer northern Italy, Emperor Frederick I – or Barbarossa – was

Charlemagne, King of Franks

defeated by an alliance of city states including Milan, Como, Cremona, Mantua, Bergamo, Brescia and Verona and supported by the pope. The alliance was established to stop Frederick I's influence over Italy.

5 11th–15th Centuries: Renaissance City States
From the 11th century the power of the city-states in northern Italy was unrivalled: the della Scala family ruled Verona and its territories; the Gonzagas ruled Mantova; the Visconti and later the Sforza ruled Milan; and Venice was a republican city-state. Gradually power was polarized and, after the Treaty of Lodi in 1454, northern Italy was dominated by the Sforzas in Milan and the Venetian Republic.

6 1559: The Spanish Grants the Duchy of Milan
Marking the beginning of over 300 years of foreign rule, Milan fell into the hands of the Spanish, who did little to solve the economic and social problems of this period.

7 1805: Napoleon Crowned King of Italy in Milan
Having invaded Austrian-ruled northern Italy in 1796 and ending 1100 years of the Venetian Republic, Napoleon took Milan and swept down the peninsula. His 20-year

Preceding pages **Boats moored in harbour, Sirmione**

reign had profound effects in Italy, which prepared the ground for the independence movement.

1861: Vittorio Emanuele I Crowned King of Italy

Lombards paid a high price for a united Italy. The Battle of Solferino, near Lake Garda, ended Austrian occupation with a partial but bloody victory. Bergamo provided 1,000 volunteers for Garibaldi's army of red shirts who sailed to Sicily and then faught back up the peninsula, securing territories for the new kingdom.

Painting of the Battle of Solferino

1919: Italy Gains South Tyrol from Austria

The border region with Austria had been in dispute since the new Kingdom of Italy defined its northern borders in 1866. The Allieds confirmed that the mod-ern-day areas of Alto-Adige and Trentino would be ceded to Italy for their part in the World War I.

1945: Mussolini's Capture

On 28 April 1945, Benito Mussolini and his mistress Claretta Petacci were executed by the Resistance in the village of Mezzegra on Lake Como. They were captured at Dongo the day before, trying to escape to Switzerland. Their bodies were taken to Milan where they were strung up in Piazza Loreto as proof of the dictator's demise.

Top 10 Roman Sites

1 Colonne di San Lorenzo, Milan
This is a series of 16 Corinthian columns dating back to the 2nd-century. Map V5

2 Fontana di Madonna, Verona
A 14th-century fountain in Piazza delle Erbe topped by a Roman statue. Map H4 • Piazza delle Erbe

3 Villa Romana, Desenzano del Garda
A sweeping 4th-century villa on the shores of Lake Garda (see p29).

4 Grotte di Catullo, Sirmione
The remains of a large 1st-century domestic villa on a promontory in Lake Garda (see p28).

5 Roman Temple, Brescia
A partly reconstructed temple, originally built in 73 AD. Map F4 • Via dei Musei

6 Teatro Romano, Verona
Restored in the 19th century, this is now a venue for music and theatre again (see p21).

7 Ruins of Imperial Palace, Milan
The remains of Emperor Maximian's palace were unearthed by World War II bombing. Map U3 • Via Brisa

8 Winged Victory Statue, Brescia
Life-sized bronze statue of Winged Victory found in the Roman temple (see p78).

9 The Arena, Verona
Verona's Roman amphi-theatre has seating capacity for 30,000 people (see p21).

10 Porta dei Leoni, Verona
This was the main entrance to Verona from the south in Republican Roman times. Map H4 • Via Leoni

Left **Stone house near Verscio** Centre **Route sign** Right **Detail of a chapel at Sacro Monte**

Walks

1 Val Cannobio, Lake Maggiore

This 7-km (4-mile) mountain-route takes you through the wooded Val Cannobio, via rugged stone hamlets to Malesco. Take the bus from Cannobio town to the start point at Cursolo, and you can pick up the train at Malesco, which is a stop-off point on the Domodossola – Locarno line *(see p62)*.

2 Sacro Monte, Orta San Giulio

Short but steep mule tracks above Orta wind up through woodland to the 21 chapels of Sacro Monte. It is a great spot for a picnic, with lovely views of the lake and Isola San Giulio *(see p12)*.

3 Orrido di Sant'Anna, Lake Maggiore

This trail (8 km/5 miles there and back) runs from Cannobio along the banks of a river, which widens to become surprisingly dramatic. At the end you reach the church

Spire of the church of Sant'Anna

of Sant'Anna, where the Sant'Anna restaurant is perched above a gorge. ◈ *Via Sant'Anna, 30 Traffiume • 0323 70682 • Restaurant Open 12–1:45pm & 7–9:45pm; closed Mon (except Jul & Aug)*

4 Centovalli, Lake Maggiore

You can pick up a number of trails from the stone hamlet of Verscio, a stop on the scenic Centovalli Railway *(see p62)* from Locarno. A good waymarked woodland path leads for 4 km (2 miles) to Streccia.

5 Greenway del Lago di Como, Lake Como

This very well-signed route follows cobbled paths and quiet lanes past the gardens of Villa del Balbianello and Villa Carlotta *(see p22)*. The total distance – from Colonno to Cadenabbia di Griante – is 11 km (7 miles), but it can also be covered in shorter sections.

6 Brunate to Torno, Lake Como

The Como funicular whisks you up to the start of this walk in Brunate. Waymarked trails lead for 12 km (8 miles) to Torno, where you can see ancient tombs carved into the rocks. You can take the boat back to Como.

7 Argegno to Ossuccio, Lake Como

Start with a cable-car ride from the pretty lakeside settlement of Argegno up to Pigra. From here you can walk for 12 km (8 miles) along old stone tracks through the Valle della Camoggia, and then via a Roman road to Ossuccio, which sits opposite Isola Comacina.

8 The Lungolago – Riva del Garda to Torbole, Lake Garda
An easy 4-km (2-mile) walk linking two settlements at the north of Lake Garda, via beaches, parkland and promenades. This blustery corner of the lake is popular with windsurfers, so you will see plenty of sporting action along the way.

A beach at Lungolago

9 Monte Isola, Lake Iseo
Explore the circumference of the traffic-free island (15 km/ 9 miles if you take paths rather than the more direct road route), or shorten the walk by picking up the ferry. You can take a detour to the hilltop Santuario della Madonna della Ceriola for mountain and lake vistas.

10 Monte Baldo, Lake Garda
Hike on established trails to Monte Baldo, above the picturesque lakeside town of Malcésine. The cable car, which does the 1,600 m (5,250 ft) in ten minutes, can save you either the upward or downward journey, depending on how energetic you are feeling *(see p57)*.

Top 10 Seasonal Sights

1 Spring Flowers
Visit in April to see the hillsides bright with primroses, periwinkles, violets, lilies of the valley and anemones.

2 Rhododendrons and Azaleas
Late spring is a wonderful time to see rhododendrons and azaleas in bloom in the formal gardens.

3 Orchids
Monte Baldo is a good spot for rare orchids, in flower from mid-April to mid-May.

4 Villa Gardens
The region's famous gardens are at their dazzling and colourful best in July and August.

5 Grape Harvest
In September the vines are heavy with clusters of grapes ripe for the *vendemmia* (grape harvest).

6 Autumn Foliage
September and October see the leaves change colour spectacularly on the wooded slopes of the lakes.

7 Funghi Porcini
Autumn is great for funghi enthusiasts, whether your interest is in eating or identifying mushrooms.

8 Chestnut Harvest
Chestnuts are collected from the wooded slopes and roasted on every street corner in October.

9 Olive Harvest
In October the olive trees are covered in shiny black olives, which are painstakingly harvested by hand.

10 Snow
During winter, the sight of snow-covered peaks soaring above the lakes is truly spectacular.

Left **Settimane Musicali di Stresa** Centre **Carnival costumes** Right **Film festival, Locarno**

🔟 Festivals

1 Settimane Musicali di Stresa e del Lago Maggiore

Since the 1960s this music festival has featured invited composers, orchestras, conductors and soloists. The venues may include Santa Caterina del Sasso, the Isole Borromeo, the Basilica di San Giulio and a 100-year-old steamship. ◎ *Last week of Aug and first week of Sep • www.stresafestival.eu*

2 Film Festival, Locarno

Locarno's annual film festival is a hallmark of diversity and international talent. The 10-day-long event includes open-air screenings in the Piazza Grande with audiences of up to 8,000 people. ◎ *Early Aug • www.pardo.ch*

3 Sant'Ambrogio, Milan

The saint's day (7 Dec) of Milan's patron saint, Saint Ambrose, is celebrated with a large crafts and gift market in the streets around Sant'Ambrogio church *(see p17)*. The day also starts the beginning of the opera season at La Scala *(see p16)*.

4 Sagra di San Giovanni, Lake Como

The Sagra di San Giovanni sees celebrations in the town of Como with music and folk festivals culminating in a big firework display on the *notte di San Giovanni*. ◎ *The nearest Sat to 24 Jun*

5 Carnival

The riotous celebrations before Lent involve dressing up with masks and lots of mischief. Lecco, Bagolino and Verona are three places especially worth heading for to enjoy traditional processions and dances. ◎ *Feb/Mar*

6 Clusone Jazz Festival

The medieval streets and Liberty summer houses of this town in the Bergamasc Valle Seriana host top international names at its established jazz festival. ◎ *Jun • www.clusonejazz.it*

7 Festa dell'uva, Bardolino

The grape harvest is celebrated in September throughout the region with wine, feasting and, often, song. In Bardolino, on the shores of Lake Garda, stalls are set up along the lakeside promenade serving hearty local food and wine. Various concerts are also organized. ◎ *Sep • www.comune. bardolino.vr.it*

Crafts market, Sant'Ambrogio

*Some sights, most shops and bars and restaurants are closed on public holidays. Public transport runs a Sunday service (**festivo**).*

8 Festa del Torrone, Cremona
Cremona sees itself as the home of *torrone*, or nougat, and celebrates the soft nutty concoction on the penultimate weekend in November. Processions in medieval costume, dances and treasure hunts are features of this festival. There are, of course, tasting sessions as well as cookery classes for children and a competition for the best recipe containing nougat. ⊘ *Last weekend in Nov • www.festadeltorronecremona.it*

Crowds at the Festa del Torrone

9 Festa del Lago, Varenna
On the first weekend of July, boats arrive at Varenna with "refugees" in medieval costume to commemorate Varenna taking in Isola Comacina's residents escaping Barbarossa in 1169 *(see p32)*. Then follows music, tasting sessions of local dishes and a spectacular display of fireworks. ⊘ *First weekend of July*

10 Santa Lucia, Bergamo
Bergamo's answer to Father Christmas is Santa Lucia: on the saint's day the town's children receive presents. From the beginning of December little wooden stalls line the streets selling toys, gifts and seasonal food and drink; they remain until 6 January to give people a chance to buy gifts from the *befana (see sidebar)*. Also celebrated in Verona. ⊘ *Dec 13*

Top 10 Public Holidays Around the Lakes

1 January
New Year's Day, or *Primo dell'anno*.

2 6 January
Epiphany; *Epifania*. The day the *befana*, or good witch, brings presents to good children and coal to naughty ones.

3 Easter Monday
Known as *Pasquetta*.

4 25 April
Liberation Day, or *Giorno della Liberazione*, celebrates the day when German forces left Italy at the end of World War II.

5 1 May
Labour Day; *Festa dei Lavoratori*

6 2 June
Republic Day, or *Festa della Repubblica*, commemorates the national referendum in 1946 when the people chose a republic instead of a monarchy.

7 15 August
The day of the Assumption of the Blessed Virgin Mary, known as "*Ferragosto*", is celebrated in Italy by shutting up shop for the day.

8 1 November
All Souls' Day, or *Ognissanto*, is the day when people go to cemetries to pay their respects to their deceased relatives.

9 8 December
The Feast of the Immaculate Conception of the Blessed Virgin Mary, or *Immacolata* is celebrated on 8 December, nine months before the Nativity of Mary.

10 25 and 26 December
Christmas and Boxing Day, or St Stephen's Day, are known as *Natale* and *Santo Stefano*.

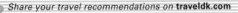

Left **Sailboats docked at a harbour** Right **Golf course in Bergamo**

Outdoor Sports

1 Kayaking
Paddling along the waters is the perfect way to get a closer view of the lakeside villas or to appreciate the soaring mountain peaks. Equipment can be hired on all the lakes but it is most easily available at the northern end of Lakes Garda and Como.

2 Horse Riding
Specialist companies arrange riding holidays in the area and tourist offices usually carry details of local companies. Many of the regions *agriturismi* have riding facilities and some arrange treks.

3 Paragliding
If you have a head for heights, floating off the sides of the mountains with great views over the waters is unmissable. Tandem and solo paragliding descents are organized from Monte Baldo above Lake Garda to Sasso del Ferro above Lake Maggiore as well as at centres on the lakes in between.

4 Sailing and Windsurfing
Watersports are on offer all around the lakes but certain spots have ideal conditions and are particularly well regarded – especially around Torbole on Lake Garda, Pino on Lake Maggiore and the northern end of Lake Como around Dervio. Even tiny Lake Iseo offers good facilities around Sarnico and Lovere.

5 Snowboarding
On the slopes around the lakes and the upper reaches of all the valleys there are pistes for snowboarding. The ski resorts in the Val Camonica, Valli d'Ossola, Monte Baldo, Mattone and around the north of Lake Garda are all good destinations.

6 Golf
There are several nine-hole courses around the lakes for a quick round. The deluxe hotels in the region also boast some of the top courses in Europe, although fees are not cheap. Menaggio on Lake Como has the oldest course in the region.
⊗ *Palazzo Arzaga, Brescia; Map F4; 030 680 600 • Circolo Golf Villa d'Este, Lake Como; Map N4; 031 200 200*
• Menaggio & Cadenabbia, Menaggio, Lake Como; Map N2; 0344 32103
• Circolo Golf Bogogno, Bogogno, nr Lake Orta; Map J5; 0322 863 794

7 Mountain Biking
Practically every resort around the lakes is in striking distance of somewhere with enjoyable mountain biking

Windsurfing on Lake Garda

territory. Whether you prefer single-track cross-country rides or exhilarating, downhill stints, there are routes throughout the region. The ferries and cable cars mean that you do not need to cover any territory twice.

Canyoning
The limestone gorges, waterfalls and glaciated features around the lakes are perfect for canyoning. This increasingly popular sport is available in numerous locations and there are various organizations in Torbole on Lake Garda, Stresa on Lake Maggiore and Gre on Lake Isco.

Hikers on Grigne, Bergamo Alps

Hiking
All around the lakes there are marvellous opportunities for walking and hiking. Paths vary from mountain treks to strolls through olive groves. Suggestions for routes are available from local tourist offices *(see p104)* or you can put together your own with combinations of boats, cable cars and trains.

Skiing
Decent downhill and Nordic skiing opportunities are available at various locations above the lakes. Attractive pistes with equipment hire could keep you entertained for a few days, but the variety and length of runs do not compete with those an hour or so further up in the Alps proper.

Top 10 Spectator Sports and Races

1 Mille Miglia
The exciting Brescia–Rome–Brescia vintage car race is held over five days in May. ◈ www.1000miglia.eu

2 Centomiglia Regatta
Go and watch the 300 or more boats that race round Lake Garda in June. ◈ www.centomiglia.it

3 Formula One
The Italian Grand Prix is held in June at this particularly speedy track just outside Milan. ◈ www.monzanet.it

4 Rowing Races
The traditional rowing races (Jun–Jul) pit local neighbourhoods against each other.

5 Palio Remiero del Lario
These rowing competitions (Sep) attract teams from throughout the region.

6 Marathon
Milan's marathon, run through the centre of the city (Oct or Nov), is one of the fastest in Italy. ◈ milanocitymarathon.gazzetta.it

7 Giro d'Italia
Watch the 100-year-old round Italy cycle race. ◈ www.giroditalia.it

8 Football
Don't miss a game from the stands of the region's numerous top-league teams. ◈ www.lega-calcio.it

9 Windsurfing Competitions
Lake Garda attracts various international windsurfing competitions such as the European championships.

10 Horse Racing
There is nothing elitist about the horse racing at Milan's hippodrome, just a fun day out. ◈ www.ippodromimilano.it

Italian Lakes' Top 10

Left **Cable car to Monte Mottarone** Right **Limone**

Cycling Routes

1 Along the Canals – Milan to the Certosa di Pavia

Head out through the southern suburbs of Milan along the tow paths heading to Pavia. The paths are not always in the best condition so the going can be slow. You will pass through villages, past bargemen's *osterie* (taverns) and beside rice fields for 20 km (12 miles) before you see the Carthusian monastery rising out of the paddy fields *(see p95)*.

2 Through the Ossola Valley

Let the train do the work to Camedo and then hire a bike and glide down through the panoramic valleys along country lanes and over viaducts. It is an easy, varied route that will take you down to Pontebrolla where you can pick up the train again.
◈ *Map K1 • www.vigezzina.com*

3 Around Malcesine, Lake Garda

The tourist office at Malcesine has put together six excellent cycle routes based around the village. They cater to all levels,

from a 90-minute trip through olive groves and along the lake to a 60 km (37 mile) freeride on Monte Baldo. Many utilize the town's spectacular cable car. The tourist office also has details of rental companies *(see p105)*.

4 Gargnano to Limone via Tignale, Lake Garda

A challenging route of around 30 km (19 miles) taking in the steep slopes and winding side roads of the western side of Lake Garda. Just north of Gargnano, a narrow road climbs up from the water to the village of Tignale (450 m/1,476 ft above the lake) offering splendid views. The road takes you through villages and wooded valleys and then higher still to Tremosine, from where it is downhill all the way to Limone. ◈ *Map R3*

5 Mincio to Peschiera del Garda

This flat 43-km (27-mile) ride takes you through the Mantovan plains along quiet asphalted back roads from Mantova to the shores of Lake Garda. It is worth stopping off at Borghetto sul Mincio to try the local speciality, *nodo d'amore* tortellini at one of the many restaurants. The Ponte Visconteo, the castles and the many water mills in the area are also worth a look before heading off along Mincio to Peschiera.
◈ *Map R5 • www.valeggio.com*

Cycling around Malcesine

6 Through the Franciacorta Vineyards

The timelessness of the Franciacorta makes it a wonderful place to explore by bike. Choose a route that lets you pop into a couple of the wine-growing estates, or enjoy a meal at one of the restaurants in the area. ⊗ Franciacorta • Map E4 • www.stradadelfranciacorta.it

Cycling through the Franciacorta vineyards

7 Around Menaggio, Lake Como

One of the many routes available from this section of the lake involves an ascent using the Argegno cable car to Pigra. From here you can climb up through alpine scenery along World War I defence lines to several mountain refuges with great views over Lakes Como and Lugano. The trip down takes you through picturesque valleys and along the old Menaggio–Porlezza train track. Contact the tourist office for detailed information and cycle hire (see p105).

8 Around Monte Isola, Lake Iseo

A relaxed alternative to the strenuous ride up to the sanctuary at the top of the Monte is the round-island trip of 9 km (5 miles). There are no private cars on the island so the well asphalted roads make for a pleasant ride. ⊗ Tourist Office: Peschiera, Monte Isola • Map F3 • 030 982 5088 • Open daily Apr-Oct, Aug: Sat & Sun; Closed Nov-Mar • www. tuttomonteisola.it

9 Monte Mottarone, Lake Maggiore

The cable car up from Stresa takes you to the panoramic viewpoint of Monte Mottarone (1,491m/4,892 ft). Bikes are available for hire at the base station or on the top of the mountain. Well-marked paths will bring you down in a few hours. ⊗ Stresa • Map J3 • 345 362 7874 • www.bicico.it

10 Cannobio to Orrido di Sant'Anna, Lake Maggiore

There is a very pleasant ride inland from Cannobio on the northwestern shore of Lake Maggiore. An 8-km (5-mile) roundtrip cycle path traces the river away from Cannobio beach through the countryside to the Orrido di Sant'Anna, a lovely gorge and a waterfall. There are places for picnics along the way, or the Ristorante Santa Anna at the falls (see p11) is good too.

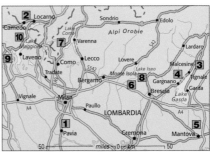

Left **Polenta** Centre **Grana Padano** Right **Casoncelli**

TOP 10 Culinary Specialities

1 Polenta
This heavy but simple staple of corn meal or grits has nourished generations of northern Italians. Traditionally served up with donkey stew, veal or creamy cheese, it is cheap and filling. These days it is often left to cool, cut into slices and served up with lake fish or grilled vegetables.

2 Lake Fish
Tinca (tench), *persico* (perch) and *luccio* (pike) are three of the most common lake fish you will come across. They are white fish with delicate flavours that are frequently offered simply grilled or baked, although they can be served in many ways including marinated or as a filling for ravioli.

3 Grana Padano
Similar to Parmigiano Reggiano, Grana Padano is a hard cow's-milk cheese often served grated on the top of pasta or rice dishes. This cheese was reputedly first created by Cistercian monks in a monastery to the south of Milan in the Middle Ages. It must be made in the Po Valley of Lombardy to earn its DOC stamp of regional authenticity.

4 Casoncelli or Casonsei
Ravioli, or pasta parcels stuffed with sausage meat and cheese, are a speciality around the towns of Bergamo and Brescia and in their valleys. Usually freshly made, the filling starter is commonly served topped with melted butter and sage leaves *(burro fuso)* and a sprinkle of Grana Padano cheese.

5 Cassoeûla
The classic way to beat the cold, foggy nights of a Milanese winter is to indulge in a heavy cassoeûla. This hearty pork and sausage casserole includes cabbage and variations of many other winter vegetables. A legacy of the Spanish occupation of the region in the 16th century, it is rarely served in restaurants these days.

6 Taleggio
A mild creamy cheese from a valley of the same name located above Bergamo, Taleggio is traditionally made in large square blocks and often served melted on polenta. The consistency varies depending on the season: in the summer months it is harder and chalky, and in the winter, far more creamy.

Taleggio cheese

Note that many restaurants and cafés do not accept credit cards.

7 Gorgonzola

This blue veined cheese from the village of the same name just outside Milan comes in two varieties: hard, crumbly and strong (which is the version usually available outside Italy) and the milder, much creamier, so called "dolce" version. Often shortened to "Zola" on menus.

8 Cotoletta alla Milanese

One of the most ubiquitous dishes on menus in Milan is *cotoletta alla Milanese*. Lightly breadcrumbed veal cutlets are fried in butter and served with a squeeze of lemon. There is usually nothing else on the plate, so if you want a side order, ask for vegetables or salad separately.

Cotoletta alla Milanese

9 Missoltini

The classic dish of missoltini is served in many restaurants along Lake Como. Small shad are dried in the sun, pressed and then salted and preserved in oil. They are commonly offered as an antipasto although they can also be served with polenta.

10 Risotto alla Milanese

The extensive paddy fields to the south of Milan provide the city with the main ingredient for its signature dish. Creamy rice dishes are common in this region but this variation is traditionally infused with golden saffron and stock made from veal shanks *(ossobuco)*.

Top 10 Restaurants for Local Dishes

1 Restel de Ferr

Game and fish top the bill-of-fare here. ◈ *Via Restel de Fer 10, Riva, Lake Garda • Map S2 • 0464 553 481 • €€€€*

2 La Streccia

Generous portions of local seasonal produce are served up with homemade bread and pasta *(see p67)*.

3 Il Ristorante di Paolo

Lombard dishes including lake specials like delicious marinated missoltini served with flare *(see p75)*.

4 Osteria Al Bianchi

Hearty Brescian staples served up in a century-old osteria in the centre of town. ◈ *Via Gasparo da Salo 32, Brescia • Map F4 • €€€€*

5 Trattoria Milanese

Traditional elegant dining rooms serving Milanese specialities including risotto and *cotoletta (see p99)*.

6 Silvio

Fresh fish from Lake Como star in dishes inspired by local culinary traditions *(see p115)*.

7 Ristorante 100km

Fine cuisine using ingredients sourced from within 100 km of the Lake Garda restaurant *(see p91)*.

8 La Botte

Snug restaurant serving Piemontese country specials including game and wild mushrooms *(see p67)*.

9 L'Ochina Bianca

A crowded little *osteria* that serves great Mantovan specialities. ◈ *Via Finzi 2, Mantova • Map H6 • 0376 323 700 • €€€€*

10 Cooperativa Città Alta

Bergamasco specialities like salami, polenta and casoncelli are served outside under vines *(see p81)*.

Left **Da Vinci's** *The Last Supper* Centre **Mantegna's** *Dead Christ* Right *Portrait of a Musician*

🔟 Works of Art

1 Leonardo da Vinci's The Last Supper
Da Vinci's masterpiece lives up to the hype. The disciples' indignance and Christ's serenity as he announces that he will be betrayed by one of them is spell binding. Notice too humble details such as the knotted tablecloth and the metal plates reflecting those used by the monks in the refectory *(see p93)*.

2 Andrea Mantegna's Dead Christ
Whether it is the perspective of this painting that pulls you in or the realism of the colouring, your eyes feel drawn to every wrinkle of the shroud. The sense of bereavement emanating from the work might stem from the fact that Mantegna's own son had recently died *(see p93)*.

3 Raphael's Angel
Painted when Raphael was just 17 for San Nicolà da Tolentino in Umbria in 1501, the retablo was damaged by an earthquake and cut up. The 19th-century collector Paolo Tosio discovered this fragment for sale in Florence; another is on display in the Louvre and a third, in Naples.
🔊 *Santa Giulia, Via Musei 81 • Map F4 • 030 377 4999 • Open Tue–Sun: 10am–6pm • www.bresciamusei.com • Adm*

Raphael's *Angel*

4 Mark Wallinger's Via Dolorosa
On permanent display at Milan's Duomo, this video installation shows Franco Zeffirelli's 1977 film *Jesus of Nazareth* in silence, with 90 per cent of the image blacked out. Its acquisition revives the tradition of Church patronage of contemporary art.

5 Rock Art, Capo di Ponte
Spread across both sides of the Val Camonica above Lake Iseo are more than 140,000 symbols and figures carved in the rock over a period of 8,000 years.
🔊 *Naquane, Capo di Ponte • Map F2 • 0364 42140 • Open Tue–Sun: 8:30am–7:30pm • www.capodiponte.eu • Adm*

6 GAMEC Collection, Bergamo
A diminutive collection of works by modern artists from Italy such as De Chirico, Morandi, Lucio Fontana and Maurizio Catalan as well as photography by Gabriel Basilico and Giacomo Manzù's sculptures. Contemporary international artists are also featured. 🔊 *Galleria d'Arte Moderna e Contemporanea, Via San Tomaso 53 • Map D3 • 035 270 272 • www.gamec.it*

7 Winged Victory, Brescia
Discovered in the Tempio Capitolino in 1826, this bronze

Most galleries and museums are closed on Mondays.

Roman statue has become the symbol of the city. It is believed that the current figure was altered in the 2nd century AD from an even older statue of Aphrodite. ✪ *Santa Giulia, Via Musei 81 • Map F4 • 030 377 4999 • Open Tue–Sun: 10am–6pm*

8 Masolino Frescoes, Castiglione Olona

Masolino da Pancale was commissioned to decorate the baptistry in this village. The frescoes, described as "an island of Tuscany in Lombardy", tell the story of John the Baptist with artful portraits and perspectives. ✪ *Map B3 • 0331 850 280*

Masolino frescoes, Castiglione Olona

9 Caravaggio's St Francis in Meditation

The star painting at Cremona's Museo Civico has all the masterful hallmarks of Caravaggio. The dark canvas shows a portrait of the saint hunched over in thought. ✪ *Museo Civico "Ala Ponzone", Via Ugolani Dati 4 • Map E6 • 0372 407 770 • Open Tue–Sat: 9am–6pm Sun: 10am–6pm • Adm*

10 Da Vinci's Portrait of a Musician

Believed by some to be a self-portrait, there is a debate over whether Da Vinci finished the painting. The wonderful detail of the face does not match the hat, clothes or hand, which are two-dimensional in comparison.

Top 10 Periods in Art and Architecture

1 Prehistoric
Ancient rock carvings document prehistoric society, its organization and beliefs.

2 Roman
Roman culture has survived in carvings, mosaics and inscriptions as well as buildings such as temples and early Christian baptisteries.

3 Romanesque
Simple architecture, triangular façades and internal frescoes are classic elements of the early Romanesque style.

4 Gothic
Gothic art was focused in the decorations of cathedrals and churches built between the 12th and 14th centuries.

5 Renaissance
Renaissance artists portrayed realism in their art; architects sought symmetry and proportion based on Classical architecture.

6 Baroque
The elaborate Baroque style was used in the Counter-Reformation drive to educate society in Roman Catholicism.

7 Neo-Classical
The late-18th and early-19th centuries saw new civic architecture with references to the Classical Greek & Roman styles.

8 Romanticism
A 19th-century revisiting of historical movements, in particular the Medieval.

9 Liberty
Italy's version of the Art Nouveau movement with its heyday between 1880–1920.

10 Futurist
An early 20th-century movement that focused on mechanization and movement; many of the main advocates of Futurism were killed in World War I.

Panoramic view of Manerba and the surrounding hills, Lake Garda

Swimming Spots

1 Lido Giardino, Menaggio, Lake Como

This complex on the northern outskirts of Menaggio offers a lake beach, some grassy patches, two pools, a children's play-ground and lovely sunbathing areas. ⊕ *Via Roma, Menaggio, Lake Como • Map N2 • 0344 30645 • Open mid-May–mid-Sep: 9am–6pm • Adm • www.lidomenaggio.it*

2 Belvedere, Iseo, Lake Iseo

This low-key lido on the edge of the lakeside town of Iseo has views across to Monte Isola. There are grassy sections and a shady picnic area, as well as a swimming pool with slides and a beach. Watersports are also offered, and equipment hire for windsurfing. ⊕ *Via per Rovato 28a, Iseo • Map E4 • 030 980 970 • Open May–Sep: 9am–8pm • Adm • www. lidobelvedereiseo.com*

3 Punta San Vigilio, Lake Garda

Even if you are not staying at the exclusive Locanda San Vigilio

hotel *(see p88)* you can still enjoy this charming little corner of the lake. The Parco Baia delle Sirene, a clean, stony pay beach, is backed by grassy olive groves. There's a picnic spot, activities for kids and refreshment kiosks. ⊕ *San Vigilio, Garda, Lake Garda • Map R4 • 045 725 5884 • Open 9:30am–8pm • Adm • www.parcobaiadellesirene.it*

4 Lido delle Bionde, Sirmione, Lake Garda

Halfway to the end of Sirmione's promontory a road leads off Via Catullo towards the town's lido. It is a good spot for swimming and sunbathing and refresh-ments are available. ⊕ *Viale Gennari 28, Sirmione, Lake Garda • Map R5 • 030 916 495 • Open May–Oct: daily 8am–midnight • Adm • www.lidodellebionde.it*

5 Manerba, Lake Garda

Located on the western coast at the south of Lake Garda, Manerba boasts 11 km (7 miles) of fine beaches with fabulous views across the lake to the distant mountains. This is a flat area with many campsites that often have their own stretches for lakeside bathing too. Manerba also has a lido with a pool and sunbathing areas.

6 Torri del Benaco Beach, Lake Garda

The north-facing, white shingle beach at the end of the promenade to the north of town is a good spot for

Punta San Vigilio, Lake Garda

cooling down. Lake views have the Trento mountains as a backdrop and there is a leafy public park on the corner with a children's playground and a little café *(see p88)*.

Shady promenade at Torri del Benaco

7 Bellagio, Lake Como

Bellagio does not have the best swimming on the lake, nor indeed is Como the cleanest of the lakes, but if you cannot bear the heat head towards the waters off the Punta Spartivento for a dip. For more facilities, check with the tourist office whether the waterfront lido – on the way to Loppia – is open *(see pp14–15)*.

8 Aqua Paradise Park, Lake Garda

Europe's largest water park at the southern end of the eastern shore of Lake Garda has something for each member of the family. There are slides and rapids, a relaxed beach and a sunbathing area as well as an exciting medley of children's theme sections complete with pirate ships, an ancient lighthouse, a fishing village, and an adventure island with an erupting volcano *(see p50)*.

9 Gravedona Beach and Lido, Lake Como

Just by the entrance into Gravedona towards the north of Lake Como is the town's beach and a small lido with two pools, a bar and great views over the lake and mountains. This is watersports territory so there are many companies offering courses and equipment for hire.

10 Cannobio, Lake Maggiore

Cannobio's beach has been awarded an annual EU Blue Flag for cleanliness for the last eight years. An attractive, spacious beach backed by shady trees, it offers various watersports such as windsurfing and sailing, although it can get crowded in peak season. To get there, follow the lakefront road, Via Magistris, north out of the centre of Cannobio just past the car park at Piazza Martiri della Libertà.

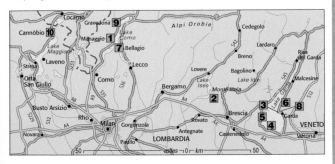

Left **Bamboo garden, Villa Carlotta** Centre **Villa Cipressi** Right **An ornate fountain in Villa Melzi**

🔟 Gardens

1 Isola Bella
Created in the 17th century, Isola Bella is famed for the Baroque excesses of its luxuriant terrace gardens. The gardens contain a Roman theatre and a system of cool grottoes, while white peacocks strut amidst statues of angels, coiffured hedges and fragrant groves *(see pp8–9)*.

2 Villa Cipressi
Lying on the edge of the village of Varenna, this villa is named after the large cypress trees in the grounds. It stands at the top of the terraced garden that leads down to the water. It's a cool intimate place with many shady nooks to relax in. ⊗ *Via IV Novembre 18, Varenna, Lake Como • Map N2 • 0341 830 113 • Open Mar–Oct: 9am–7pm daily, closed Nov–Feb • Adm*

Statues framing the fine view, Isola Bella

3 Villa Carlotta
The romantic gardens of Villa Carlotta on Lake Como are a delightful mix of terraces, statues, fountains, staircases and splendid views. The spring flowering of 150 different species of rhododendrons and azaleas is a beautiful sight, as are the ancient cedars, sequoias and plane trees. The Japanese-inspired bamboo garden with rare species and calming waterfalls is a soothing retreat *(see p22)*.

4 Villa del Balbianello
The approach from the water is unforgettable, with steps leading up a scissor staircase, past statues and topiary to the pretty panoramic loggia. The grounds here are a delightfully idiosyncratic blend of colourful flowery borders, geometrical hedges and huge oaks, cypresses and magnolias *(see p23)*.

5 Villa Melzi
A short walk from Bellagio, Villa Melzi was one of the first gardens on the lakes to be designed in the informal English style, in 1808. The immaculate lawns stretch down to the water's edge with palms, cypresses and plane trees framing the wonderful views. ⊗ *Lungolario Manzoni, Bellagio, Lake Como • Map N4 • 339 457 3838 • Open daily Apr–Oct: 9:30am–6:30pm • Adm*

Members of the UK National Trust or Royal Horticultural Society, will get free or reduced entrance to several of the gardens.

Villa Taranto
Scottish sea captain Neil McEacharn created a botanical garden, complete with dahlias and azaleas, a bog garden, a huge pond floating with water lilies and an Italianate garden. When he died in 1964, he was buried in a mausoleum in the grounds. ◈ Verbania Pallanza, Lake Maggiore

The verdant botanical garden at Villa Taranto

• Map J3 • 0323 404 555 • Villa Taranto landing stage • Open daily Apr–Nov 8:30am–6:30pm; closes 5pm in Nov • Adm • www.villataranto.it

Isole di Brissago
Just offshore in the Swiss section of Lake Maggiore, the tiny island of San Pancrazio was transformed into a splendid botanical garden in 1856 by the wealthy Baroness Antoinette de St. Léger. A staggering variety of species on display, including Japanese banana trees, Chinese tea plants and shady Canarian palms (see p11).

Isola Madre
With its sweeping lawns, home to an array of exotic flora, mature trees, shaded paths and fine views, it is no wonder that French novelist Gustave Flaubert

(1821–80) declared Isola Madre to be his favourite island. ◈ Stresa, Lake Maggiore • Map J3 • 0323 30 556 • Ferry from Stresa, Baveno or Pallanza • Open daily mid-Mar–mid-Oct 9am–5:30pm • Adm • www.borromeoturismo.it

Heller Garden
Founded by Arturo Hruska in 1912 and formally known as the Giardino Botanico Hruska, this garden features flora from around the world, including orchid meadows and giant ferns. It is now decorated with sculptures and installations. ◈ Via Roma 2, Gardone Riviera, Lake Garda • Map Q4 • 336 410 877 • Open Mar–Oct 9am–7pm • Adm • www.hellergarden.com

Villa Serbelloni
Commonly speculated to be the site of Pliny the Younger's Roman villa, the villa gardens are some of the quietest on the lakes. There are lovely views of the point where the three branches of Lake Como meet from the belvedere in the wooded upper garden. Near the house, the 18th-century formal section is split into curved terraces with topiary and statues (see p22).

Left **Pizza** Centre **Windsurfing, Torbole** Right **Castello Sforzesco**

Children's Attractions

1 Steamer Trip, Garda
The steam boats operating on Lake Garda are a wonderful way to chug about the lake. The summer-only service uses beautifully maintained boats dating from 1908. The steamer has a more reduced service than other ferries, but manages to take in most of the larger resorts ⊗ Map R4 • Adm • www.navigazionelaghi.it

2 Swissminiatur, Melide
Backed by snow-covered mountains, this beautifully landscaped model village in Switzerland offers scale reproductions of over 100 Swiss buildings and Milan's Duomo. There is also a model railway and working boats and cable cars zipping around. ⊗ Via Cantonale Melide 6815, Switzerland • Map L3 • 4191 640 10 60 • Melide station • Open mid-Mar–end Oct 9am–5pm (last adm 4:30pm) • Adm • www.swissminiatur.ch

3 Gardaland
Located in the southeastern corner of Lake Garda, Italy's largest theme park offers

Gardaland theme park

a fun day out for most ages with roller coasters, space rides, an Egyptian area and zones for younger kids too. ⊗ Castelnuovo del Garda, 37014 • Map R5 • 045 644 9777 • Adm • www.gardaland.it

4 Aqua Paradise Park, Garda
All types of water slides and rides, shoots, jumps and rapids here keep the older children busy. A full-sized galleon, pirates and a water playground add to the fun. There are also calmer pools where you can relax while the family splash around, and paddling pools for babies. ⊗ Fossalta 1, 37017, Lazise sul Garda • Map R4 • 045 696 9900 • Open early May–late Sep 10am–6pm; in high season and at weekends closes at 7pm • Adm • www.canevaworld.it

5 Cablecar, Monte Baldo
The revolving panoramic pods on Monte Baldo's cablecar (confusingly called a "tramway" locally) travel up the mountain from the town of Malcesine on the eastern shore of Lake Garda. As well as the dizzying fun and the magnificent views en route, the top of the mountain offers numerous hiking, mountain-biking and parasailing opportunities. ⊗ Navene Vecchia, 12–37018, Malcesine • Map S3 • 045 740 0206 • Mid-Mar–Nov: 8am–6:45pm; winter closes 2 hrs earlier • Adm • www.funiviedelbaldo.it

Children get free or discounted entry to sights in Italy. Most public transport is free for under 4s; under 12s pay 50 per cent.

6 Windsurfing, Torbole
Torbole on the northeastern tip of Lake Garda is a windsurfer's paradise. The calm waters of the mornings are perfect for novices, while when the breezes stir up there is enough to challenge anyone. Kiteboarding and sailing classes and equipment are also available; courses and boards are easily found. www.torbole.com

7 Castello di Vezio
Perched at the top of the cliff with a wonderful panorama over Lake Como, these castle ruins are ten minutes of impossibly steep steps up from the Varenna landing jetty. A good outdoor bar-restaurant, weekend falconry displays, a fossil exhibition and some ghostly figures dotted around the grounds add to the fun (see p23).

8 Pizza and Gelati
Few kids will turn their nose up at food that they are allowed to eat with their fingers. On pizzas, margherita (mozerella and tomato) or marinara (tomato only) toppings should work for fussy eaters, while the more adventurous can have a field day with the myriad of other options. Gelati artigianali (homemade ice creams) fill the gaps between meals perfectly. A visit to GROM

Giardini Pubblici, Milan

gelateria is a good way to experience tasty flavours made from organic ingredients. www.grom.it

9 Giardini Pubblici, Milan
Play areas for different ages, a lake with carp and turtles, a merry-go-round and, at weekends, dodgem cars, pony rides and a ride-on miniature train – all manage to fit into Milan's central park while still leaving space to kick a football under the trees or have a picnic in the shade.
Porta Venezia, Milan • Map X1 • Metro Palestro, Turati & Porta Venezia

10 Castello Sforzesco, Milan
Once drilling on the parade ground has been exhausted, the collection of weaponry and armour in the castle museum will keep some children entertained for hours; others might be taken by the slightly incongruous Egyptian collection (see p17).

Above **Corso Como 10 Café, Milan**

TOP 10 Elegant Bars & Cafés

1 Gold Bar, Milan
Since Dolce and Gabbana opened this temple to all things golden just round the corner from their headquarters, it has become the hangout for those who like to see and be seen in Milan. Upstairs there is a formal restaurant and downstairs an all-day bistro, a café and a bar for evening lounging. *Via Carlo Poerio, Milan • 02 757 7771*

2 Bar, Grand Hotel des Illes Borromees, Lake Maggiore
Sip a "cool and clean" martini at the bar in the opulent surround-ings here just as Hemmingway's hero Frederick Henry did in the novel *A Farewell to Arms*, or indeed Ernest Hemmingway himself on his many visits to the hotel *(see p112)*.

3 Cocktail Bar, Villa Cortine Palace Hotel, Sirmione
The polished walnut bar and the intricate parquet flooring of this bar at the lakeside Villa Cortine on Sirmione's promontory creates a refined atmosphere for a brandy or two. *Via Grotte 6, Sirmione, Lake Garda • 030 990 5890*

4 Just Cavalli Café, Milan
On the edges of the Parco Sempione, this über-styled world is done up with low-level sofas and floor cushions around a huge canopy, lit by candles and torches and with a live lounge sound track. *Viale Camoens, Torre Branca, Milan • 02 311 817*

5 H-Club Diana Bar, Milan
A stylish bar that has been an essential part of Milan's nightlife over the last decade and popular with visiting fashionistas. *Sheraton Diana Majestic Hotel, Viale Piave 42, Milan • 02 205 81 • www.sheratondianamajestic.com*

6 Corso Como 10 Café, Milan
A most Milanese of institutions, this is a designer shop, art gallery, bookshop, boutique hotel and café-bar all rolled into one, at the north end of Corso Garibaldi. *Corso Como 10, Milan • www.10corsocomo.com*

7 Terrace Bar, Villa d'Este, Lake Como
The Terrace Bar in this historic hotel, located on the dreamy shores of Lake Como, serves up tasty snacks and drinks with beautiful views. *Via Regina 40, Cernobbio, Lake Como • 031 3481 • www.villadeste.it*

Sunny Terrace Bar at the Villa d'Este, Lake Como

212 Bar Code, Bergamo

8 The bars and tearooms under the porticoes of the Sentirone have been the place for a morning coffee or an evening *aperitivo* for over 100 years. 212 Bar Code is an updated alternative with sleek lines and glossy white interiors. Relax and watch the Bergamo *passeggiata* (evening stroll) from the comfort of the outside tables. ◈ *Via Sentirone 37, Bergamo* • *035 428 4646*

Chic interiors of Al Mascaron, Verona

Al Mascaron, Verona

9 Just across the water from the town centre in the attractive piazza overlooked by San Zeno Maggiore, this popular bar is a fashionable choice for a drink or snack from early evening until the small hours. There is live music on Wednesday evenings. ◈ *Piazza San Zeno 16, Verona* • *045 59 7081*

Taverna San Vigilio, Lake Garda

10 This is an idyllic corner of Lake Garda: a handful of tables are put out on the tiny horseshoe-shaped harbour next to the stone *locanda* (inn). Sip a glass of wine to the sound of crickets chirping in the neighbouring olive groves. ◈ *Punta San Vigilio Garda, Lake Garda* • *045 725 6688* • *www.locanda-sanvigilio.it*

Top 10 Drinks

1 Franciacorta Sparkling Whites
The award-winning bubbly of choice around the lakes is Italy's only sparkling wine produced according to the classic Champagne method.

2 Valtellina Superiore
A strong red wine that perfectly accompanies a plate of mountain salami.

3 Prosecco
A sparkling white wine – usually dry – produced in the Veneto region.

4 Grappa
Warming firewater made from the leftovers of the wine-making process – skins, stalks and all.

5 Bardolino
A light, ruby red wine produced on the western shore of Lake Garda that complements the region's fish dishes well.

6 Limoncello
Originating on the Amalfi coast and served chilled, this sweet lemon liquor with a kick is a common after-dinner drink around the lakes.

7 Bellini
This popular cocktail of prosecco (sparkling wine) and peach juice was originally invented in Venice.

8 Campari Bitter
Try a shot of one of Milan's most famous inventions.

9 Riviera del Garda Bresciano
The DOC wines *(see p54)* from the eastern shores of Lake Garda include strong reds, a straw-coloured white and a light ruby rosé.

10 Lugana White
An aromatic white wine made on the southern shores of Lake Garda.

Left **Gabbani delicatessen, Lugano** Centre **San Babila, Milan** Right **Quadrilatero d'Oro, Milan**

🔟 Shopping

Galleria Vittorio Emanuele II, Milan

1 Galleria Vittorio Emanuele II
A precursor to the modern mall, this Milan landmark is a perfect spot for shopping away from the city's infamous heat or drizzle. Prada, Gucci, Ferrari, Borsalino and other top names are all nestled here under the leaded glass roof (see p16).

2 Gabbani Delicatessen
A wonderful array of cheeses and cured meats are on display at this famous shop tucked away in a lane off Piazza della Reforma in Lugano. The fruit and vegetables are top quality as are the breads and pastries. ◈ Via Pessina 12, Lugano • Map L2 • 91 911 3080

3 Quadrilatero d'Oro
This rectangle of smart streets at the heart of Milan features an A to Z of the world's top fashion labels. Collections change with the seasons and there are sales from the end of July and the beginning of January respectively (see p17). ◈ Map X1

4 Around San Babila
With a centuries-old tradition of furniture-making and industrial engineering, it is not surprising that 1950s Milan became one of the world centres of contemporary furniture and design. Spacious showrooms offer anything from a three-piece suite to a more suitcase-friendly table light or mezzaluna. ◈ Map X3

5 Boutiques
Lake Como's rarefied industry (see pp14–15) leads to displays of rack-upon-rack of colourful silk ties and scarves. Designs often follow the latest collections of top fashion designers that the silk factories are also working for. Check for origins as some cheaper goods are imported.

6 Wine Outlets
Low prices, expert advice and tasting sessions are offered at wine estates, cooperatives and agriturismos. The Denominazione di Origine Controllata e Garantita (DOCG) and Denominazione di Origine Controllata (DOC) names are Valcaleppio and Scanzo from around Bergamo; Valpolicello, Bardolino and Soave from near Lake Garda; plus Franciacorta's sparkling wines. Good drinkable wines are also made on the sunny slopes around all the lakes.

7 Alprose Chocolate Factory
The little industrial town of Caslano lives off perhaps Switzerland's greatest export:

chocolate. The Alprose chocolate factory has a museum explaining the origins and processes, and a factory shop sells the whole range at bargain prices. ⊗ *Alprose, Via Rompada 36, Caslano-Lugano • Map L2 • 91 6118 888 • Museum: Open Mon–Fri 9am–5:30pm Sat–Sun 9am–4:30pm • Adm*

Omegna
The unpretty sprawl of Omegna at the northern end of Lake Orta is home to Bialetti, the best Italian coffee-pot maker and the quirky designer products of Alessi. Both factory stores have good bargains. ⊗ *Alessi: Via privata Alessi 6, Crusinallo di Omegna & Bialetti: Piazza Siro Collini, Omegna • Map A3*

Street Markets
As a source of locally produced cheeses, salamis and smoked hams, the weekly street markets throughout the region are unbeatable. The quality of produce here is excellent and prices fair.

Fresh produce at a street market

Factory Outlets
The traditional textile industry of northern Lombardy has evolved in recent decades to meet the needs of Milan's fashion industry. Small, family-run factories produce much of what makes it onto the catwalks. The outlets dotted around the region sell off surplus stock and can offer some genuine bargains.

Top 10 Buys

1 Designer Furniture and Lighting
Bag a bit of Milanese design with classics such as Gio Ponte chairs or Castiglione lights.

2 Coffee Pots and Cork Screws
Bialetti's La Dama is an Italian classic, while Alessi's colourful plastic designs make perfect take-home gifts.

3 Leather Goods
Although not specifically from this part of the country, Italy is always a good place for well-priced leather goods, shoes and boots.

4 Cigars
A long thin Virginia cigar, the Brissago originates in the resort of the same name on Lake Maggiore.

5 Cheeses
Head for Bellinzona's annual cheese market in October or any delicatessen selling local Gorgonzola, Provolone, Grana or Taleggio.

6 High-End Fashion
As an international centre of haute couture Milan has the world's top labels.

7 Outlet Fashion
Top designer labels reduced to a third of the price or shelves of oddly shaped mismatches – outlet shopping is a happy lucky dip.

8 Silk
Como-made silk goods are usually top-quality and in the latest styles.

9 Wine from Small Vineyards
Support local initiatives and save money in the process.

10 New Season Olive Oil
The Mediterranean climate affecting pockets of the lakes region is perfect for growing olives – southwestern Lake Garda in particular.

Left **A ferry docked on Lake Maggiore** Right **View from Lake Como ferry**

TOP10 Great Journeys

1 Lake Maggiore Express
This round-trip excursion includes a long ferry trip along Lake Maggiore, a fabulously scenic railway ride and a speedy train. The journey crosses from Italy into Switzerland, and you can start and end wherever you want on the lake and stop off as frequently as you please. Tickets are available all around the lake and can be valid for more than one day (see pp62–3).

2 Locarno Cable Car and Chair Lift
After taking the funicular railway up to the Santuario della Madonna del Sasso, perched on a rock above Locarno, head for the glass-sided cable cars that glide you up the incline to Cardada (1,350 m/4,429 ft). From this point there are awe-inspiring views across the peaks and lakes of the region. A 10-minute walk through the woods from here leads you to a chairlift to Cimetta (1,672 m/5,485 ft), seemingly at the very top of the world.
⊗ Map L1 • 41 (0)91 735 3030 • Adm
• www.cardada.ch

3 Lake Como Ferry
There are few better ways of enjoying the exquisite views of the lakeside villas and old fishing villages of Lake Como than from the ferry as it pulls in and out of the little harbours. The Centro Lago triangular trip takes in three of Lake Como's most delightful villages, chugging at a stately pace and is never too packed.
⊗ www.navigazionelaghi.it

4 Lakeside Walk from Lugano to Gandria
Just outside Lugano (see p65), the little settlement of Castagnola is the start for the Sentiero di Gandria footpath. The path goes through the attractive Parco degli Ulivi to the appealing lakeside village of Gandria, 5 km (3 miles) away. The park extends up the hillside that becomes Monte Brè, and is lush with olive trees, cypresses, oleander bushes and scented shrubs. ⊗ Map L2

5 Boat to Isola Bella
Reaching Isola Bella by water either from Baveno, Stresa or Verbania is unforgettable. As the

Arriving at Isola Bella

Remember to take your passport for trips between Italy and Switzerland.

Breathtaking views from the Monte Baldo cable car

Baroque terraces of the extra-vagant gardens glide closer, the ferry circles the island to approach the landing stage, offering glimpses of secret corners of the gardens and palace *(see pp8–9)*.

Bergamo Funicular
Although the ride takes just seven minutes, this is still the best introduction to Bergamo's Città Alta. The narrow train squeezes up from the lower town past 19th-century villas and through pretty gardens right to the heart of Bergamo's medieval upper town *(see p25)*.

Treno Blu
Summer Sundays see this private train leave Bergamo for Lake Iseo, around 30 km (19 miles) away, where it is met by a ferry that waltzes you around the lake with stopovers on the island of Monte Isola before heading back to Bergamo *(see p78)*.
◈ www.ferrovieturistiche.it • Operates Mar–Oct • 030 7402851

Monte Baldo Cable Car
State-of-the-art revolving cabins offer panoramic views across Lake Garda as you rise up 1,600 m (5,249 ft) from Malcesine. Split into two sections, the route takes ten minutes up to Monte Baldo from where there are cycling and hiking routes galore as well as skiing and paragliding opportunities *(see pp38–9)*.
◈ www.funiviamalcesine.com

Como e Lugano Boat Trip
The *Como e Lugano: Due Laghi per Sognare* (Two Lakes to Dream of) trip starts from Como with a fast train to Lugano, then a boat on Lake Lugano to Porlezza, a bus back through the hills to Menaggio on Lake Como and a scenic boat trip back to the start. The journey can be made in reverse and the ticket is valid for two days. ◈ www.navigazionelaghi.it

Cycling in the Mountains
In comparison with the crowded lakeside resorts and villages, the hills and mountains above the lakes in Northern Italy are generally little visited. Cyclists are spoilt for choice with mountain paths, rough tracks and winding roads. Enjoy the views as you head down through vineyards, olive groves and lemon cultivations *(see pp40–41)*.

AROUND THE ITALIAN LAKES

Lake Maggiore
60–67

Lake Como
70–75

Bergamo, Brescia and
Lake Iseo
76–81

Lake Garda and
Around
84–91

Milan and Southern
Lombardy
92–99

ITALIAN LAKES' TOP 10

Left **Interiors, Rocca Borromeo** Centre **Garden at Villa Taranto** Right **Pallanza, Verbania**

Lake Maggiore and Around

THE WESTERNMOST OF ITALY'S GREAT LAKES, *Maggiore's proximity to the Alps and its temperate climate have made it a favourite retreat for holidaying northern Europeans for centuries. These conditions have also helped create Maggiore's biggest draw – its many luxuriant gardens. From the palm-tree lined promenades to the formal terraces of the Borromean Islands, the Alpine gardens and the immaculate lawns of the Grand Hotels, Lake Maggiore is in bloom throughout the year. The mountains and valleys leading away from the turquoise water offer a myriad of sights and activities to complement lazy times by the lakeside. Just over Mount Mottarone, to the southwest, lie the tranquil and glittering waters of Lake Orta, the most westerly of the lakes, with one significant draw in the sun-kissed village of Orta San Giulio.*

View from Teatro Massimo, Isola Bella

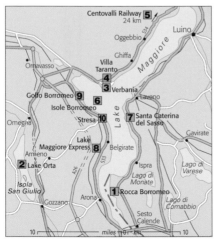

Sights

1. Rocca Borromeo
2. Lake Orta
3. Verbania
4. Villa Taranto
5. Centovalli Railway
6. Isole Borromeo
7. Santa Caterina del Sasso
8. Lake Maggiore Express
9. Golfo Borromeo
10. Stresa

Preceding pages **Serbelloni lane, Bellagio, Lake Como**

Rocca Borromeo

1 This medieval castle was bought from the Visconti by the current owners, the Borromeo family, in 1449. Wonderfully preserved, it enjoys a strategic position above the town of Angera, with extensive vistas across the southern reaches of the lake *(see p64)*. Highlights include the

Decorated celings, Rocca Borromeo

lofty Torre Principale and the vaulted Sala di Giustizia (Law Court), a huge room decorated with 13th-century frescoes. ✪ *Map J4 • 0331 931 300 • A walk uphill from Angera landing stage • Open mid-Mar–mid-Oct: 9am–5.30pm • Adm • www.borromeoturismo.it*

Lake Orta

2 Narrow little Lake Orta is a serene backwater in comparison with its neighbours although it too has been a tourist destination for several centuries. The northern tip is rather industrialized but the southern end of the lake is hardly touched. Frequently referred to as the "pearl" of the lake, Orta San Giulio, an enchanting village on the western shore, is one of the most lovely places in the whole region *(see pp12–13)*.

Verbania

3 Halfway up on the western side of the lake, Verbania is a 20th-century renaming of the adjacent lakeside villages of Suna, Pallanza and Intra, although they retain very different identities. Intra is the transport hub for train, bus and cross-lake ferries. Pallanza is the pick of the two: a low-key resort with a southerly aspect and sublime views across the lake. ✪ *Tourist Office: Corso Zanitello 6, Pallanza • Map J3 • 0323 503 249 • www.verbania-turismo.it*

Villa Taranto

4 Captain Neil McEacharn bought this villa and grounds in Verbania in 1931 to fulfil his ambition of creating a botanical garden. The result is a heady mix of scents and colours in flowering borders, woodlands, greenhouses and formal gardens with fountains and waterfalls. There is a vast collection of exotic plants, 300 types of dahlias and equatorial lily pads. ✪ *Verbania Pallanza • Map J3 • 0323 404 555 • Open daily Apr–Oct: 8:30am–6:30pm; Nov: 8:30am–5pm • Adm • www.villataranto.it*

Picturesque Pallanza, Verbania

Around the Region – Lake Maggiore and Around

Ferry Service

Lake Maggiore is serviced by an efficient ferry service divided into four sections: the lower zone to Angera; the central zone including Stresa and Pallanza; the northern zone from Cannero to the border; and the Swiss basin. A trip from Arona to Locarno takes 4 hours. See landing stages and www.navigazionelaghi.it for more details.

Fountain in the garden of Isola Bella

Centovalli Railway

Opened in 1923, the 52-km (32-mile) stretch of railway between Domodossola in Italy and Locarno in Switzerland passes through craggy cliffs, wooded valleys, over vertiginous bridges and past half-forgotten villages, vineyards and waterfalls. As well as a wonderful daytrip, you can also break your journey as frequently as you wish to explore by bike or on foot. ✎ Map K1 • 0324 242 055 • Adm • www. vigezzina.com; www.centovalli.ch

Isole Borromeo

The four tiny islands between Pallanza and Stresa are the main destination of most visitors to Lake Maggiore; only three are open to the public. Isola Bella (see pp8–9) is the most famous: an extraordinary Baroque creation of palace, lakeside grottoes and formal terraced gardens. Isola Madre is the largest island but less ostentatious with a modest villa and beautiful gardens. Isola dei Pescatori (or Superiore), a pretty fishing village, is the only island not still owned by the Borromeo family. ✎ Map J3 • 0323 30 556 • Ferry from Stresa, Baveno or Pallanza • Open daily mid-Mar–mid-Oct: 9am–5:30pm • Isola Bella: Adm; Isola Madre: Adm; • Guided tours available; book one day in advance • www. borromeoturismo.it

Santa Caterina del Sasso

Built onto the sheer face of the rock on the eastern shore, this pretty stone hermitage is only visible from the water. Founded in 1170 when a certain Alberto Besozzi survived a shipwreck here by praying to St Catherine of Alexandria, it has been added to over the centuries to include two convents, a church and a chapterhouse. ✎ Map K3 • Open daily Apr–Oct: 8:30am–noon & 2:30–6pm; Nov–May: 9am–noon & 2–5pm; Feb: weekends only • www.provincia.va.it/santacaterina

Santa Caterina del Sasso

Lake Maggiore Express

A highlight of any Lake Maggiore holiday, this splendid initiative is a combination of public transport using ferry and rail through both Italy and Switzerland. The trip can take from six hours to a couple of days with as

You will need your passport to enter Switzerland at the northern end of the lake.

many stops as you fancy. Included are a boat trip on Lake Maggiore, the Centovalli Railway between Locarno and Domodossola and a fast train back to the water *(see p10)*.

9 Golfo Borromeo

The Golfo Borromeo is a term used to describe the bulge on the western shore of the lake home to Maggiore's best-known towns and attractions. The popular resorts of Stresa and Baveno *(see p64)* face Verbania across the bay dotted with the three Borromeo Islands. Watercrafts shuttle between the shores and islands including the car-ferry across the lake to Laveno on the eastern shore *(see p64)*.

Cobbled street lined with shops, Stresa

10 Stresa

Stresa's heyday was in the 1920s and 30s when Europe's aristocracy arrived by train at this little resort with breathtaking views over the Borromean Islands and the lake beyond. The waterfront Grand Hotels continue to offer nostalgic grandeur. The location is ideal for daytrips to the islands or up to the top of Mount Mottarone (1491-m/4,892-ft) in a cable car.
⊛ *Tourist office: Piazza Marconi, by the ferry jetty • Map J3 • 0323 31 308 • Open daily: 10am–12:30pm & 3–6:30pm; Nov–Feb closed Sat & Sun • www.distrettolaghi.it; www.stresa-mottarone.it*

A Day on the Lago Maggiore Express

Morning

🕐 Boarding the **Lago Maggiore Express** will mean a comfortable start from the **Stresa** landing stage with the 11:15am ferry heading for **Locarno** *(see p65)*. You can have a three-course lunch on board (book before departure) and relax with a glass of wine as you pass the landmarks of the lake. Once past the **Isole Borromeo** the lake narrows round the final squiggle and you pass Cannero and Cannobio *(see p64)* to the Swiss border.

Late Afternoon

Past the Isole di Brissago at the northern tip of Lake Maggiore, the elegant resort of **Locarno** is an inviting place to pass an hour or so wandering off the cobbled alleyways off Piazza Grande and relaxing with an ice cream at one of the pavement cafés before catching the 4:12pm train to Domodossola.

The breathtaking **Centovalli Railway** section of the trip offers magnificent panoramas as you pass through mountain crevices, ancient chestnut woods and over gravity-defying bridges before crossing the border back into Italy and arriving at the Italian town of Domodossola an hour and a half later. The town centre offers various traditional trattoria if you want an early dinner or perhaps just an *aperitivo* and a plateful of nibbles from one of the bars with outdoor seating. The last Cisalpino train leaves Domodossola at 9:55pm for the 40-minute trip back to **Stresa**.

Left **Picturesque Cannero** Centre **Interior of Rocca Borromeo, Angera** Right **Arona**

Towns and Villages

1 Ranco
Located on the southeastern corner of Lake Maggiore, Ranco is a quiet little place with an attractive waterfront. Visit the Ogliari Transport Museum, which has numerous historical forms of transport. ⊗ *Ogliari Transport Museum, Via Alberto 99 • Map J4 • Open Apr–Sep 10-11:30am & 3– 5:30pm; Oct–Mar: 10–11:30am & 2–4:30pm • 033 197 5198*

2 Orta San Giulio
Enchanting Orta has lanes of stone buildings opening on to a cobbled piazza with views across the lake of an islet and wooded hills beyond *(see p12)*.

3 Luino
Popular for its Wednesday market, Luino is also the birthplace of Bernardino Luini – one of Da Vinci's followers. Luini's frescoes can be seen in the cemetery church *(see p11)*.

4 Laveno
Lakeside Laveno is a useful transport hub and docking point for the regular cross-lake ferry to Intra on the western shore. ⊗ *Map K3 • www.laveno-online.it*

5 Baveno
The tightly knit centre of lanes in Baveno opens on to the lakeside with a delightful Art -Nouveau landing-stage. ⊗ *Tourist Office: Piazza Dante Alighieri 14 • Map J3 • 0323 92 4632 • Open Mon–Sat 9am–12:30pm & 3–6pm; more restricted hours in winter*

6 Cannobio
This lovely low-key resort surrounded by a mix of small hotels and campsites has a good beach and a pretty village centre of steep lanes. ⊗ *Map K2*

7 Arona
The lake's most southerly town has a pretty cobbled centre and good rail connections. Climb up inside the 35-m (115-ft) high statue of San Carlone, just out of town, and peer out of his ears for dizzying views across the lake. ⊗ *San Carlo • Map J4 • 0322 249 669 • Open daily mid-Mar–Nov 8:30am–12:30pm & 2–6:30pm; Nov–mid-Mar: Sat & Sun 9am–12:30pm & 2–5pm*

8 Mergozzo
Around the 9th century, silt from the River Toce cut Mergozzo off from Lake Maggiore. Since then this sleepy village has fronted its own splash of water – tiny Lake Mergozzo. ⊗ *Map J3*

9 Cannero
This quiet resort enjoys a suntrap on the western shore, and is lush with citrus fruit and olive groves that add a touch of the Mediterranean. ⊗ *Map K2*

10 Angera
Opposite Arona at the southern end of the lake, pleasant Angera is dominated by the fascinatingly complete medieval fortress, Rocca Borromeo *(see p61)*. ⊗ *Tourist Office: Piazza Garibaldi 10 • Map J4 • 0331 960256*

Remember to carry your passport to cross the border between Italy and Switzerland.

Left **Ascona's waterfront** Centre **Lush garden in Lugano** Right **Locarno's central square**

🔟 Into Switzerland

1 Locarno
Famous for its camellias and summer film festival, Locarno has a grand arcaded central square where the whole town seems to congregate on summer evenings *(see p11)*.

2 Valle Maggia
Just outside Locarno, Valle Maggia offers a network of valleys leading up to unspoilt Alpine peaks, ideal for walks or rides. ✆ *Map K1 • www.vallemaggia.ch*

3 Santa Maria degli Angeli, Monte Tamaro
Just past the flood plains at the top of the lake, gondolas rise up from the Rivera to Monte Tamaro. Here, by the top station with breathtaking views, stands Mario Botta's Santa Maria degli Angeli (1997), an intimate memorial chapel. ✆ *Map L2 • www.montetamaro.ch*

4 Centovalli Railway
A stunning railway line that runs from Locarno in Switzerland, squeezing through narrow valleys and over ancient bridges to Domodossola in Italy. Also available as part of the Lago Maggiore Express *(see p62)*.

5 Ascona
This south-facing town with its attractive waterfront promenade looking out over the Isole Brissago is a very popular resort with German-speaking Swiss tourists *(see p11)*.

6 Bellinzona
Low-key Bellinzona is home to fine architecture and a stupendous trio of castles granted UNESCO World Heritage Site status in 2000. ✆ *Tourist Office: Piazza Nosetto • Map C1 • 091 825 21 31 • Open Mon–Fri 9am–6:30pm; Sat 9am–noon • www.bellinzonaturismo.ch*

7 Alto Ticino
The Alto Ticino, a place of lonesome valleys and soaring skies, has two ancient passes – San Gottardo and San Bernadino – that linked north and south Europe in times past. ✆ *Map C1 • www.sanbernardino.ch*

8 Lugano
The lively and chic city of Lugano, the halfway point between Lakes Maggiore and Como, sits proudly on its own lake. ✆ *Map L2 • 091 913 32 32 • www.lugano-tourism.ch*

9 Gandria
A romantic hideaway east along the lake from Lugano, Gandria tumbles down the hillside into the water. Terrace cafés offer idyllic views. ✆ *Map M2*

10 Monte Generoso
Capolago on the southern shore of Lake Lugano is the access point for the rack railway up Monte Generoso (1,705 m/ 5,595 ft). The panorama takes in Milan and Turin as well as Lakes Como and Maggiore. ✆ *Map M3 • www.montegeneroso.ch*

Left **Private ferries, Stresa** Centre **Cobbled street, Cannobio** Right **Garden, Isola Madre**

Beauty Spots

1 Stresa's Promenade
The manicured lawns of the Grand Hotels that line Stresa's waterfront lead down to the palm-tree lined promenade or *lungolago*. From here there are views of the small crafts buzzing between the Isole Borromeo *(see p63)*.

2 Atrio di Diana, Isola Bella
The entry into the palace gardens is marked by a lush courtyard complete with fountains and a statue of the goddess Diana *(see p9)*.

3 Isola San Giulio
Settle down on one of the wooden jetties on this diminutive island and gaze over to the slopes of chestnut trees on the westerly shore or back at the enchanting village of Orta San Giulio *(see p12)*.

4 Cannobio's Cobbled Streets
The steep cobbled streets back from the waterfront in Cannobio remind us that this is the edge of mountain territory. The heavy stone buildings shade from the sun and protect from the winter wind *(see pp10-11)*.

5 Valle Cannobina
Narrow roads wind up to the unspoiled green hillsides, dotted with small hamlets and working farms of Val Cannobina – an area ideal for hiking, trekking and cycling *(see p34)*.

6 Gardens of Isola Madre
The extensive gardens with their pergolas of wisteria and ancient Cashmere Cyprus offer a tranquil retreat for this otherwise busy corner of the lake *(see p62)*.

7 Villa della Porta Bozzolo, Casalzuigno
A wonderful retreat from the lakes, this 15th-century country residence has immaculate land-scaped Italian grounds – complete with a secret garden. ◈ *Varese • Map K3 • 0332 624 136 • Open Mar–Sep: Wed–Sun 10am–6pm; Oct, Nov, mid-Feb closes 5pm; Jan & Dec closed • Adm • www.fondoambiente.it*

8 Rocca Borromeo, Angera
Dominating the southern section of Lake Maggiore, this majestic castle sits atop a spur of rock surveying all for miles around *(see p61)*.

9 Alpinia Botanic Garden
Halfway up Mount Mottarone above Stresa, these gardens offer the most splendid views across Lake Maggiore to the Alps. ◈ *Piazzale Lido 8, Alpino, Stresa • Map J3 • 0323 30 295 • Cable car Stresa–Alpino–Mottarone • Open Apr–Oct 9:30 am–6pm • Adm • www.giardinoalpinia.it*

10 Santa Caterina del Sasso
Strung out across a rocky ridge 18 m (60 ft) above the water and visible only from the lake, the diminutive monastery of Santa Caterina del Sasso affords lovely views *(see p62)*.

Above **Warm interior of La Streccia, Cannobio**

TOP 10 Places to Eat

1 Il Sole
Located on the waterside, this warm family-run hotel and restaurant offers local delicacies with innovative mixtures, flavours and textures. ◈ *Piazza Venezia 5, Ranco • Map J4 • 0331 976 507 • €€*

2 Dei Cigni
Top-quality creative cuisine is served at this informal trattoria. Reserve one of the few terrace tables overlooking the Borromeo Bay and enjoy homemade pasta with rabbit and pistachio or fresh eel carpaccio. ◈ *Vicolo Dell'Arco 1, Verbania • 0323 558 842 • €*

3 Hotel Verbano
Find a place on the waterside terrace after the crowds have left and tuck into delicious traditional local offerings. ◈ *Via Ugo Ara 2, Isola dei Pescatori • Map J3 • 0323 30 408 • Closed Nov–Mar • €€€*

4 La Botte
A cosy *osteria* with a mountain feel in the heart of Stresa's pedestrian lanes, offering hearty Piemontese cuisine including game, polenta and fresh pasta. ◈ *Via Mazzini 6, Stresa • 0323 30 462 • Closed Thu • €*

5 Villa Crespi
Award-winning cuisine combining southern Italian flavours with local produce is beautifully presented in the elaborate dining rooms here. ◈ *Via Fava 18, Lake Orta • 0322 911 902 • Closed Mon & Tue L, Jan–Feb • €€€€€*

6 La Piemontese
An old fashioned restaurant in the heart of Stresa, offering good traditional food in slightly formal surroundings. ◈ *Via Mazzini 25, Stresa • 0323 30 235 • Closed Mon, Dec, Jan • €€€*

7 Piccolo Lago
Another of the area's new wave of restaurants serving excellent innovative cuisine in a glass restaurant suspended over Lake Mergozzo. ◈ *Via Filippo Turati 87, Fondotoce, Lake Mergozzo • 0323 586 792 • Closed Mon & Tue • €€€€€*

8 La Vecchia Arona
The menu here flaunts a mixture of traditional pasta dishes and some lighter, more unusual, reinterpretations. ◈ *Via Marconi 17, Arona • 0322 242 469 • Closed Fri • €€€*

9 La Streccia
Hidden away in a tiny alleyway leading back from the waterfront, this rustic trattoria offers warming Piemontese dishes – using mushrooms, meats and cheeses – at moderate prices. ◈ *Via Merzagora 5, Cannobio • 0323 70 575 • Close Tue • €€*

10 Al Boeuc
Tucked away just off Piazza Motta, this bar serves a fine selection of wines and platters of cold meats and cheeses. There are also a couple of tables in the shady lane outside. ◈ *Via Bersani 28, Orta San Giulio • Map J4 • 0322 915 854 • Closed Tue • €€*

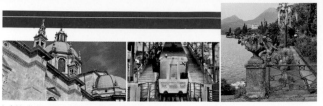

Left **Vaulted roof of the Duomo** Centre **Como Funicular** Right **Villa Monastero**

Lake Como and Around

THE THIRD LARGEST, AND THE DEEPEST OF ALL THE ITALIAN LAKES, *Lake Como* is 50 km (30 miles) long, 4.5 km (3 miles) across at its widest point and the southern section is divided into two branches. The lake is named after its main town at the southernmost tip but it is also known locally as Lario. Visitors have been flocking to these sapphire waters for centuries. In Roman times, both Pliny the Elder and the Younger had houses here and for the past 300 years, European aristocracy and industrialists have lined the shores with their villas. At the end of the 19th century, the Grand Tour encouraged elegant hotels, and these days the lake attracts a comfortable mixture of Italians and foreigners, holiday makers and glitterati.

Houses and villas at the shores of the lake

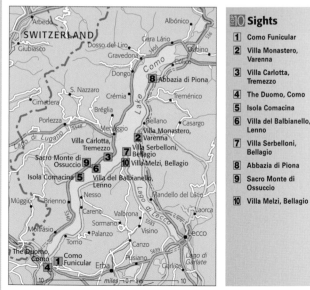

🔟 Sights

1. Como Funicular
2. Villa Monastero, Varenna
3. Villa Carlotta, Tremezzo
4. The Duomo, Como
5. Isola Comacina
6. Villa del Balbianello, Lenno
7. Villa Serbelloni, Bellagio
8. Abbazia di Piona
9. Sacro Monte di Ossuccio
10. Villa Melzi, Bellagio

Preceding pages **Lake Como, Bellagio**

Como Funicular
1 This quaint little funicular has been hauling passengers up the steep hill from Como to the village of Brunate since 1894. It passes through a tunnel and inches past resplendent villas and magnificent gardens on a one-rail system at an incline of 55 per cent, offering wonderful views of the lake and town on the way. At the top there are cafés, restaurants and the start of various signposted walks *(see p14)*.

Villa Monastero, Varenna
2 As the name suggests, Villa Monastero was built on the site of a former monastery. Rebuilt as a holiday retreat in the 16th century, these days it is used as a conference centre. The gardens have an astounding collection of plant species, and are dotted with fountains, statues and temples. The villa has unrivalled views looking towards Pescallo on the Bellagio peninsula *(see pp22–3)*. ◎ *Via IV Novembre • Map N2 • Open mid-Mar–Apr & Oct: 10am–5pm; May–28 Sep: 9am–7pm • Adm • www.villamonastero.eu*

Sculptured gardens of Villa Carlotta, Tremezzo

Exterior of the Duomo, Como

Villa Carlotta, Tremezzo
3 In 1843, the impossibly romantic 16th-century Villa Carlotta was given by Princess Marianne of Nassau, wife of Albert of Prussia, to her daughter Carlotta as a wedding present. The Neo-Classical villa flaunts period interiors alongside paintings including, appropriately, *Eros and Psyche* by Francesco Hayez (1791–1882). The sweeping terraced gardens leading down to the waterfront are lush with a blaze of azaleas in spring as well as banks of camellias and ancient cedars and sequoias. ◎ *Via Regina 2 • Map N3 • 0344 404 05 • Open daily mid-Mar & mid-Oct–mid-Nov: 10am–4pm (building is closed from noon–2pm), Apr–Sep: closes 6pm • Adm • www.villacarlotta.it*

The Duomo, Como
4 This attractive cathedral, located in the centre of Como, is the happy result of changes in artistic styles in the 300 odd years it took for it to be completed. Its lofty dimensions and soaring arches are Medieval Gothic, the apses and tapestries inside are Renaissance and the 18th-century cupola topping the building is wonderfully Baroque. Dozens of colourful stained-glass windows brighten up the otherwise gloomy interior of the church; the oldest dates from the 15th century. Look out for the small frog carved in 1507 to the left of the north door, the Door of the Frog *(see p14)*.

Around the Region – Lake Como and Around

Isola Comacina

Just off Argegno on the western shore, Isola Comacina is the only island on the lake, and one with a significant history. It was a pre-Roman settlement, a refuge for local warring fractions in the Middle Ages and, finally, sacked by Como in 1169. San Giovanni is the only standing church here but there are the ruins of at least five more scattered around.

Map N3 • 031 821 955; 335 707 4122 • Boat from Sala Comacina: 9am–7pm; return ticket €5, 7pm until the end of service at the Locanda return ticket €6 • www.comacina.it

Villa del Balbianello, Lenno

This 18th-century villa enjoys one of the best positions on the lake with breathtaking views framed by the Grigne mountains. The house holds the collections of the last owner, the Italian explorer and mountaineer, Guido Monzino,

the first Italian to climb Everest. The lush gardens, a testimony to the temperate climate, cascade down the terracing to the water. Scenes from *Star Wars Episode II* were filmed here in 2000 and *Casino Royale* in 2006 *(see p23).*

Villa Serbelloni, Bellagio

Built in 1605, Villa Serbelloni, set in extensive grounds on the hilltop above Bellagio, is now a conference centre for the Rockerfeller Foundation. Guided tours take visitors around the immaculate terraced gardens that offer panoramic views of all three branches of the lake, quiet grottoes and host of cyprus and olive trees. Note the nearby hotel with a similar name *(see p22).*

Abbazia di Piona

Perched on a peninsula on the upper reaches of the eastern shores of Como, this 12th-century monastery sits on the remains of a 7th-century church. The peaceful cloisters are the centre of the complex and the stone columns are covered with a profusion of carvings. The Cistercian monks who now look after the place make and sell a potent herb liqueur by the main gate. *Colico • Map N2 • 0341 940 331 • Ferry to Olgiasca • www.cistercensi.info*

Picturesque surroundings of Villa Balbianello, Lenno

For details of walks around the lakes see pp34–5.

Chapel, Sacro Monte di Ossuccio

9 Sacro Monte di Ossuccio

Nestling among olive groves with great views over the waters, this is one of nine UNESCO World Heritage *Sacri Monti* (Sacred Mountains) in northern Italy. A world away from the crowds, the series of fourteen chapels leading up to the sanctuary tells Bible stories with tableaux of life-size wooden statues. Seventeenth-century Franciscan monks created the site over 70 years to educate locals in teachings of what is now called Catholicism rather than the Protestant Reformation ideas sweeping the region at the time. ◈ *Ossuccio • Map N3 • 0344 55 211 • www.comunicare.it/luoghi/luoghi/ossuccio.htm*

10 Villa Melzi, Bellagio

The grounds of Villa Melzi stretch from the outskirts of Bellagio to the fishing village of Loppia to the south. A Neo-Classical building with wonderful gardens and a lake, the villa was built in 1810 as the summer residence of Francesco Melzi d'Eril, vice president of the Italian Republic under Napoleon. The estate includes an orangery, banks of rhododendrons and azaleas as well as a Japanese garden. ◈ *Lungolario Manzoni, Loppia • Map N3 • 339 457 3838 • Gardens open daily Apr–Oct: 9am–6pm • Adm • www.giardinidivillamelzi.it*

A Day on Lake Como

Morning

After breakfast at Como, head down to the jetties in front of Piazza Cavour to catch the 10am ferry service up the lake. Settle down for a 2-hour cruise along the western branch of the lake, pulling in and out of picturesque villages on both shores. At the private jetty for **Villa Carlotta** *(see p71)* hop off and head up to one of the most fabulous properties on the lake. If you are interested in the 19th-century interiors in the villa, pop inside, otherwise wander at will through the heady and luxuriant gardens. Stop for lunch at the Orangery Café or the picnic spot if you came prepared.

Afternoon

After lunch catch the fast boat over to **Bellagio**, *(see pp22–3)* just 6 minutes away, to wander the steep, cobbled lanes for a bit of shopping. There are no bargains here but browsing the selection of silk goods, wood carvings and gourmet offerings is a fun way to explore the village. If you have got the energy, one more quick ferry trip will get you away from the crowds; catch the Centro Lago car-ferry service for 15 minutes over to Varenna. Turn right off the jetty and wander along the waterfront walkway to the tiny harbour, outdoor cafés and homemade ice cream shop. Relax and enjoy the views of the lake and late-afternoon sun. Catch the express boat service (1-hour) to be back in Como in time for dinner (Note that you might need to cross to Menaggio first, depending on the timetable).

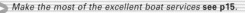

Make the most of the excellent boat services see p15.

Left **Town square, Cernobbio** Right **Menaggio**

Towns and Villages

1 Gravedona
The main town in northern Lake Como, Gravedona is home to the lovely 12th-century church Santa Maria del Tiglio. ◈ *Map N1*
• *www.gravedona.it*

2 Cernobbio
Just beyond Como, at the foot of Monte Bisbino (1,325m/ 4,347 ft), small town Cernobbio is most famous as the home of the Grand Hotel and gardens of the Villa d'Este *(see p112)*. ◈ *Map M4*

3 Lecco
At the foot of the eastern fork of Lake Como, the small town of Lecco is famous as the birthplace of 19th-century author, Alessandro Manzoni. ◈ *Map P4*
• *Tourist Office: Via Nazario Sauro 6, 23900 Lecco* • *0341 295 720* • *www. turismo.provincia.lecco.it*

4 Argegno
The small town of Argegno gives the first glimpse of the impressive mountain ranges to the northeast and, with a quick zip up neighbouring Pigra (900 m/2,950 ft) in the funicular, there are even more breathtaking views of the lake. ◈ *Map M3*

5 Nesso
Down below road level, halfway between Como and Bellagio, the pretty stone village of Nesso is divided by one of the many gorges in this area and crossed by a delightful Roman hump-backed bridge. ◈ *Map N3*

6 Torno
A charming village on the eastern shore, Torno has terraced walkways and a pretty harbour overlooked by the Romanesque church of San Giovanni. ◈ *Map M4*

7 Brienno
Tucked away from the main road on the western shore, this atmospheric hamlet has narrow walkways that weave between the houses where the lake water laps up against the ancient stone. ◈ *Map M3*

8 Bellano
Bustling Bellano is a world away from the sleepy resorts further south. A spectacular gorge, or *orrido*, with metal walkways over the roaring river is the main draw. ◈ *Map N2* • *338 524 6716* • *Open 21 Mar–18 Apr: 10:30am– 12:30pm; 19 Apr–27 Sep: 10–12:30pm*

9 Menaggio
Plump in the middle of the western shore of the lake, only 20 km (12 miles) from the Swiss border and on all the major ferry routes, Menaggio is an excellent base for exploring the area *(see p23)*. ◈ *Map C2*

10 Varenna
Half asleep in the warm afternoon sun, Varenna is the main attraction on the western shore of Lake Como, even though it is a low-key village with just a handful of sights and hotels *(see p23)*.

Price Categories

For a three-course meal for one, with half a bottle of wine (or equivalent meal), taxes, and extra charges.

€	under €30
€€	€30–€40
€€€	€40–€50
€€€€	€50–€60
€€€€€	over €60

Above **Plush interior of Mistral at Villa Serbelloni, Bellagio**

🔟 Places to Eat

1 Il Ristorante di Paolo
A convivial place on Menaggio's main square offering great food and an excellent wine list. 🐾 *Largo Cavour 5, Menaggio • Map N2 • 0344 32 133 • €€*

2 Crotto dei Platani
The romantic lakeside tables are unbeatable in summer while winter sees the restaurant move inside to the homely *crotto*, or cave. The menu mixes traditional lake cuisine with innovative dishes. 🐾 *Via Regina 73, Brienno • Map M3 • 031 814 038 • €€€€*

3 La Cucina della Marianna
Excellent home cooking is on offer at this charming family-run *albergo-ristorante*. 🐾 *Via Regina 57, Griante, Cadenabbia • Map N3 • 034 443 111 • Closed Mon, Tue-Sun L • €€€*

4 La Colombetta
In the heart of Como, this restaurant is a maze of handsome dining rooms. A good wine list accompanies the gourmet cuisine. 🐾 *Via Diaz 40, Como • Map M4 • 031 262 703 • €€€€*

5 Locanda dell'Isola Comacina
A beautiful island location is the setting for this quirky experience. The set menu hasn't changed since the restaurant opened in 1947 and the meal is rounded off with a "fire ceremony". 🐾 *Isola Comacina • Map N3 • 0344 55 083 • Open Jul–Sep daily; closed Nov–Mar, Tue • €€€€€*

6 Vecchia Varenna
Sit at a table virtually over the lake and enjoy dishes from a tasty menu, including game and good versions of the local fish dishes. 🐾 *Contrada Scoscesa 10, Varenna • Map N2 • 0341 830 793 • Closed Mon, Dec–Jan • €€€*

7 Silvio
A bright dining room with wonderful lake views complement the fish-based menu at this wonderful restaurant run by the Ponzini family for five generations. 🐾 *Via Carcano 12, Bellagio • Map N3 • 031 950 322 • Closed Tue • €*

8 Il Cavatappi
The best meals in the area are served in this simple trattoria tucked down an alleyway. 🐾 *Via XX Settembre, Varenna • Map N2 • 0341 81 349 • Closed Wed • €€€*

9 Barchetta
Fine gourmet cuisine is served on a pretty vine-covered terrace, while hearty staples and crispy pizzas feature on the menu downstairs. 🐾 *Salita Nella 13, Bellagio • Map N3 • 031 951 389 • Closed Tue & Nov–Mar • €€€€*

10 Mistral
Italy's top molecular cooking expert, Ettore Bocchia, has earned a Michelin star for the creations served at this restaurant. 🐾 *Grand Hotel Villa Serbelloni, Via Roma 1, 22021 Bellagio • Map N3 • 031 956 435 • Open Jun–Sep: Thu–Mon, closed Wed, Dec–Feb L • €€€€€ • www.ristorantemistral.com*

➔ *A hotel-cum-restaurant is called* **albergo-ristorante** *in Italian.*

Left **Santa Maria Maggiore** Centre **Monte Isola, Lake Iseo** Right **Caffè del Tasso, Piazza Vecchia**

Bergamo, Brescia and Lake Iseo

BERGAMO STANDS NORTHEAST OF MILAN *at the foothills of the Alps guarding northern Italy's main east-west roads and railway links. An immediately likeable and prosperous place, Bergamo is best known for its attractive upper town, perched atop a hill. Lake Iseo, 20 km (12 miles) away, is one of the lesser-visited but prettiest of the smaller lakes in the region, with the attractive glacier valley of Val Camonica stretching up to Switzerland behind. Bergamo's closest rival in prosperity, industry, football and just about everything else is the historic town of Brescia, 43 km (27 miles) east. The relationship between the two has never been easy, but for a visitor the experiences are very different, with Brescia's Roman heritage complementing Bergamo's medieval splendours. On summer weekends and during August, both towns empty out to the lakes and surrounding mountains.*

Tempio Capitolino, Roman sites, Brescia

🔟 Sights

1. San Vigilio, Bergamo
2. Accademia Carrara, Bergamo
3. Monte Isola, Lake Iseo
4. Funicular, Bergamo
5. Rock Art, Capo di Ponte
6. Museo Donizettiano, Bergamo
7. Santa Maria Maggiore, Bergamo
8. Roman Sites, Brescia
9. Cruises, Lake Iseo
10. Piazza Vecchia, Bergamo

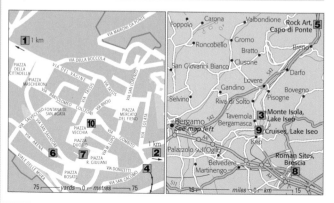

For more details see www.provincia.bergamo.it/turismo

1 San Vigilio, Bergamo

The tiny neighbourhood of San Vigilio, at the very top of Bergamo's upper town, has always been a half-forgotten corner of the city. At the beginning of the 19th century, a cable car *(see p25)* was opened to attract daytrippers to the

Cycling on Monte Isola

neighbourhood. Little has since changed. There are a few restaurants and a bar and spectacular views across elaborate gardens. The ruins of the castle here have been turned into a park with subterranean Venetian defence tunnels to be explored. ◈ *Map D3*

2 Accademia Carrara, Bergamo

Bergamo's main art gallery is based on the private collection of Giacomo Carrara, a merchant collector who bequeathed it to the city at the end of the 18th century. Masterpieces include works by Botticelli, Pisanello, Bellini, Lorenzo Lotto and Velázquez. Closed for restoration until at least 2013; some works are on display in Piazza Vecchia. ◈ *Piazza Carrara 82 • Map D3 • 035 399 677 • Open Tue–Sun 10am–1pm & 2:30–5:30pm • Adm • www.accademiacarrara. bergamo.it*

Funicular, Bergamo

3 Monte Isola, Lake Iseo

Rising up out of the middle Lake Iseo, Monte Isola is Europe's largest lake island. A wooded plug of rock, 3-km (2-miles) long and 600-m (1,970-ft) high, it only has a couple of villages and is topped by the Sanctuary of Madonna della Ceriola. Bike hire is available and there are good paths for walking or cycling. It is a popular Italian holiday spot and lunch spot with restaurants dotted along the shoreline, a couple of campsites and some low-key hotels.
◈ *Tourist Office: Via Peschiera Maraglio • Map F3 • 030 982 5088 • www.navigazionelagoiseo.it • www.tuttomonteisola.it*

4 Funicular, Bergamo

Bergamo boasts two separate funicular systems. The best known trundles from Via Vittorio Emanuele II in the lower town through the city walls to Piazza Mercato delle Scarpe in the upper town. Completed in 1887, it covers 85 m (280 ft) with a maximum incline of 52 per cent. The lesser-known route runs from Porta Sant'Alessandro in the upper town to San Vigilio, Bergamo's highest point. Since 1912 it has been carrying people up to the restaurants, cafés and the ruined castle on a 90-m (280-ft) long track at an incline of 22 per cent *(see p25)*.

Treno Blu

During summer on Sundays, a privately-run train leaves Bergamo station for the scenic trip to Paratico on tiny Lake Iseo. Boats connect here to take you over to Iseo and the panoramic Monte Isola. Details are available from tourist offices or at *www.ferrovieturistiche.it*

Santa Maria Maggiore

Rock Art, Capo di Ponte

The Val Camonica, north of Lake Iseo, is littered with pre-historic rock carvings spanning several thousand years. Recognized as a UNESCO World Heritage Site, the Parco Nazionale delle Incisioni Rupestri (National Rock Carving Park; follow the yellow signs from the main road) is an open-air site with carvings recording local life over a 1,000 years of civilization up to the Bronze Age in the 4th century. Stick figures show religious ceremonies, agricultural work, jewellery and even a cart and a blacksmith *(see p44)*.

Museo Donizettiano, Bergamo

Fans of the opera composer Gaetano Donizetti, born in Bergamo in 1797, should visit this museum illustrating his life and works. Donizetti is best known for his melodramatic piece *Lucia di Lammermoor*, but comic pieces like *Don Pasquale* also made him popular. The museum is housed in an upper town *palazzo* with a entrance courtyard and 19th-century frescoes. Original letters, instruments and scores belonging to the maestro are on display *(see p25)*.

Poster of Gaetano Donizetti

Santa Maria Maggiore, Bergamo

This church on the Piazza del Duomo in Bergamo's upper town is a trio of delights. The outside is a good example of Lombard Romanesque with a Gothic portal guarded by marble lions while the 16th-century interior is a Baroque extravaganza of guilded stucco and frescoed decoration. Next door, the Renaissance funerary chapel for Bartolomeo Colleoni, a Venetian mercenary and his daughter, is an array of pink and white marble, frescoes and bas reliefs *(see p24)*.

Roman Sites, Brescia

The 1st-century monastery of Santa Giulia, now the Museo della Città, was built on the residential area of the Roman town of Brixia – modern-day Brescia. The remains of Roman villas have been excavated and are on view *in situ* with lovely mosaic floors and wonderfully preserved frescoed walls. Also in the museum is Winged Victory, a bronze statue of Aphrodite, which was found in the Tempio Capitolino (AD 73) the semi con-structed remains of which line the road to the museum. 🕲 *Tempio Capitolino: Map F4; Open Tue–Sun 10:30am–6pm; Santa Giulia: Open Jun–Sep: Tue–Sun 10am–6pm; Oct–May: 9:30am–5:30pm • Adm: Santa Giulia*

Cruises, Lake Iseo
To complement the regular ferry service around Lake Iseo, there are a number of round-the-lake cruises that run in the summer months. Typically, the cruises last an hour or two and circumnavigate Monte Isola and the two tiny private islands on the lake – San Paolo and Loreto. Other options involve taking in the higher or the lower reaches of the lake. There is even a nightime cruise with dinner and drinks on board. 🕲 *www.barcaioli-monteisola.it; www.navigazionelagoiseo.it*

Piazza Vecchia

Piazza Vecchia, Bergamo
The impressive Piazza Vecchia is all that an Italian town square should be. Restaurants and cafés line the edges while the Neo-Classical Palazzo della Ragione stands solidly at one end facing the medieval Palazzo della Ragione at the other. There is a fountain at the centred square and the 17th-century Torre Civica (or Campanone) towers over the ensemble, chiming away every half hour. 🕲 *Torre Civica: Map D3; Open Oct: Tue–Fri 9:30am–7pm, Sat & Sun 9:30am–9:30pm; Nov–Feb: Tue–Sun 9:30am–5:30pm, Sat & Sun 9:30am–4:30pm • Torre Civica: Adm*

Half-a-Day in Città Alta, Bergamo

Morning

🕙 Grab a table in the sun in **Piazza Vecchia** for a late breakfast or morning coffee and simply take in the splendour of the square. The main sights of the city are a stone's throw away behind the Palazzo della Ragione, in Piazza Duomo. After your fill of Baroque exuberance in **Santa Maria Maggiore** and the Cappella Colleoni, if you have a head for heights, climb up the Torre Civica for panoramic views and ear-splitting chimes. From the square, bear left along via Colleoni towards the Cittadella, perhaps popping into the Teatro Sociale, at number 4, or any of the boutiques or delicatessens that line the route. Dive down any of the cobbled lanes that take your fancy; it will be easy to make your way back.

Afternoon

Just off Colle Aperto, through Porta San'Alessandro on the right, is the funicular up to **San Vigilio** *(see p77)*; make sure you have change for a ticket from the machine. At the top, wander along the road in either direction for sweeping views over Bergamo and the plains. Visit the park in the old castle ruins for a little shade. The fresh wood-oven pizzas and delicious local dishes at **San Vigilio** *(see p81)* are an excellent choice for lunch. Take in the lovely views over the valley, and plan a route to walk down through Porta San Giacomo to the lower town.

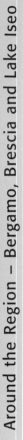

Left **Garden, San Pellegrino Terme** Right **Iseo Town**

🔟 Best of the Rest

1 San Pellegrino Terme
This spa town, north of Bergamo, has a sprinkling of Art Nouveau buildings and lush gardens. 🌐 Map D3 • Spa open May–Sep • www.comune.sanpellegrinoterme.bg.it

2 Franciacorta Wine Region
Famous for its sparkling wine, vineyards and restaurants, the hills here are dotted with sleepy villages, monasteries and patrician villas (see p41). 🌐 Map E4 • www.stradedelfranciacorta.it

3 Contemporary Art Collection, Villa Panza
On the outskirts of Varese, the lovely Villa Panza boasts a collection of top-quality contemporary American art, including some site-specific installations from James Turrell and Dan Flavin. The works juxtapose beautifully with antique furniture and original décor. 🌐 Piazza Litta 1, Varese • Map L4 • 0332 283 960 • Open Tue–Sun 10am–6pm, closed Jan • Adm, free for National Trust members • www.fondoambiente.it/beni/villa-e-collezione-panza.asp

4 Iseo Town
Drop by the local produce market here on Tuesday or Friday mornings. 🌐 Map E4

5 Val Camonica
The ski centres of Borno, Pontedilegno and Montecampione offer modern facilities and in summer, the slopes are wonderful for hiking. 🌐 Map F3 • www.adamelloski.com, www.cooptur.it

6 Teatro Sociale, Bergamo
This oval three-tiered wooden theatre fell into disrepair in the 20th century and has only recently reopened (see p24).

7 Clusone, Val Seriana
This little town is dotted with pretty Liberty villas and has an attractive medieval centre of steep, cobbled streets. 🌐 Map E3 • www.turismoproclusone.it

8 Watersports, Lago d'Iseo
Canoeing, windsurfing and sailing are available at many centres on the lake including Gré, just south of Lovere. 🌐 Sportaction, Solto Collina, Gré, Iseo • 340 984 3097, • Map F3 • 0364 536 254 • www.monticolo.it

9 Galleria Taldini
Luigi Taldini bequeathed his art collection to Lovere in 1817 in memory of his son who died here. 🌐 Via Taldini 40 • Map F3 • 035 962 780 • Open May–Sep: Tue–Sat 3–7pm, Sun 10am–noon & 3–7pm; Apr & Oct: Sat 3–7 pm, Sun 10am–noon & 3–7pm

10 Santa Maria della Neve
There are frescoes within this church, just outside Pisogne on Lake Iseo. 🌐 Pisogne • Map F3

Left **Cooperativa Città Alta** signage Right **The airy loggia of Donizetti**

TOP 10 Places to Eat

1 Vasco da Gama
The menu at this restaurant in the heart of Brescia offers welcome alternatives to the usual staples. Fish is a speciality. ◈ *Via Musei 4, Brescia • Map F4 • 030 375 4039 • Closed Tue • €€*

2 San Vigilio
Delicious pizzas are served bubbling from the wood-burning stove at San Vigilio. There are lovely views from the balcony. ◈ *Via San Vigilio 34, Bergamo • Map D3 • 035 253 188 • €€*

3 Il Paiolo
This friendly trattoria serves good-value home cooking of traditional Italian staples and stands in one of the prettiest squares in Iseo. ◈ *Piazza Mazzini 9 • Map E4 • 030 982 1074 • Closed Tue • €*

4 Osteria di Via Solata
Bergamo's only Michelin star is proudly held by this elegant upper town *osteria*. The service is friendly and the fine food and wine served with knowledge and enthusiasm. ◈ *Via Solata, Città Alta, Bergamo • Map D3 • 035 271 993 • €€€€€*

5 Donizetti
Do accompany your platter of local cheeses or four-course meal here with a glass of recommended wine. In summer, tables are outside under the atmospheric loggia. ◈ *Via Gombito, 17/a, Città Alta, Bergamo • Map D3 • 035 242 661 • €€*

6 I Due Roccoli
An elegant choice up in the hills about 5 km (3 miles) outside Iseo. A limited range of dishes using seasonal ingredients is offered. Rooms are also available. ◈ *Colline di Iseo, Via Silvio Bonomelli, Iseo • Map E4 • 030 982 2977 • Closed Nov–mid-Mar • €€€*

7 Vineria Cozzi
This refined but friendly place offers gourmet food and a superb selection of local and national vintages. ◈ *Via Colleoni 2, Città Alta, Bergamo • Map D3 • Closed Wed • 035 238836 • €€€*

8 Osteria Al Bianchi
Traditional Brescian staples including *malfatti* (spinach and ricotta dumplings) and *brasato d'asino* (donkey stew) are served in this old-world *osteria*. ◈ *Via Gasparo Da Salò 32, Brescia • Map F4 • 030 292 328 • Closed Tue & Wed • €*

9 Due Stelle
Quality Brescian cooking is served in this eatery. Main courses are meat-based, including local specialities of horse-meat stew and roast rabbit. ◈ *Via Faustino 48, Brescia • Map F4 • 030 375 8198 • Closed Sun D & Mon • €€€*

10 Cooperativa Città Alta
Sit at one of the vine-covered tables in the garden and tuck into servings of Bergamo's mountain cooking. ◈ *Vicolo Sant'Agata 19, Città Alta, Bergamo • Map D3 • 035 218 568 • €*

Around the Region – Bergamo, Brescia and Lake Iseo

Left **Castle, Malcesine** Right **Boats docked at the harbour at Gargnano**

Lake Garda and Around

LAKE GARDA IS AN AREA OF CONTRASTS. *The terrain of the northern section is more rugged, with deep water and strong winds that make this part of the lake ideal for watersports. To the south, the edges of the lake are gentler, with stony beaches and pretty vine-covered hills with lemon and olive groves. Garda is the most easterly of the main Italian lakes and the largest, measuring about 51 km (31 miles) in length. The water is the cleanest and the temperature far milder and more Mediterranean in nature than it should be for its latitude. This adds up to make Lake Garda the most visited of the Italian Lakes; the waterside roads and villages can get thoroughly jammed in season but further afield there are idyllic valleys to explore as well as the appealing historic town of Verona.*

Beach, Lake Garda

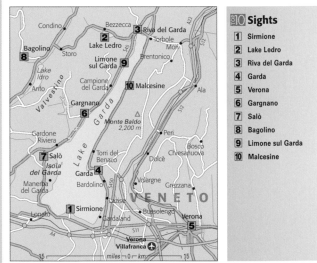

Sights

1 Sirmione
2 Lake Ledro
3 Riva del Garda
4 Garda
5 Verona
6 Gargnano
7 Salò
8 Bagolino
9 Limone sul Garda
10 Malcesine

Preceding pages **Tiled rooftops of houses, Lake Maggiore**

Sirmione

Jutting out from the southern shore on a little promontory, Sirmione is a pretty, historical town perfect for day trips, although it is exceptionally busy in summer. The natural spa here, originating from the Boiola spring, made this a popular spot in Roman times. The town's main sight is the impressive Rocca Scaligera, a medieval castle dating back to the 13th century (see p29).

Lake Ledro

In peaceful contrast to its busy neighbour, Lake Ledro is a little mountain tarn 8 km (5 miles) from the northwestern end of Lake Garda. Activities here include fishing, watersports such as sailing and canoeing, and biking. The southern shores hold a small archaeological museum covering the excavations of Bronze Age stilt dwellings. ◎ Tourist Office: Via Nuova 9, Pieve di Ledro; 0464 591 222 • Map R2 • Lake Ledro Museum: Via al Lago, Molina di Ledro; 0464 508 182 ; Open Jul & Aug 10am–6pm, Sep–Nov 9am–5pm; Closed Dec, Jan & Feb, Mar–Jun closed Mon • Adm • www.vallediledro.com; www.palafitteledro.it

Riva del Garda, Piazza III Novembre

Rocca Scaligera, Sirmione

Riva del Garda

Located at the northern tip of the lake, Riva is sheltered under the overhanging cliffs of Monte Rochetta. One of the larger towns on the waters, Riva was a fashionable resort at the beginning of the 20th century. It was under Austro-Hungarian rule and only passed into Italian hands at the end of World War I. The large lakefront piazza is framed on three sides by 14th-century porticoed buildings, behind which the town's walls contain the narrow streets of the pedestrianized quarter. The moated castle, or Rocca, to the east marks the beginning of Riva's gardens and long stretch of beaches. It is also the centre for various sports activities on the lake. ◎ Tourist Office: Largo Medaglie d'Oro 5 • Map S2 • 0464 554 444 • www.gardatrentino.it

Garda

An attractive resort town built around a small bay, Garda has a long beach and a broad lakeside promenade lined with terrace cafés. The tight network of lanes are just set back from the water. There are some ancient stone buildings as well as many shops selling souvenirs and cheap leather goods. On the other side of the main road, villas, hotels and guesthouses stretch up the winding hillside. ◎ Tourist Office: Piazza Donatori di Sangue 1, Garda • Map R4 • 045 627 0384

Lake Ferries

Lake Garda can be visited at a relaxed pace aboard the lake's many ferries, hydrofoils and catamarans. There are also car-ferries crossing the lake between Toscolano-Maderno and Torri del Benaco. Details available at landing stages, tourist offices, and by telephoning *800 551 901*. Visit *www.navigazionelaghi.it* for timetables.

Detail of the Duomo door, Salò

Verona

Famously the setting for Shakespeare's *Romeo and Juliet*, this historic town, 20 km (12 miles) from the lake, is one of the most elegant places in the region, boasting an attractive pedestrianized centre. Spectacular Roman ruins such as the Arena nestle among the cobbled lanes cheek-by-jowl with medieval palaces, a magnificent castle in the Castelvecchio and a tempting array of trattorias and wine bars *(see pp20–21)*.

Gargnano

This small strip of a village is an absolute joy: there is nothing much in the centre except a pair of tiny harbours, a church and some waterside houses but the atmosphere is delightful. D.H. Lawrence wrote *Twilight in Italy* here in 1912 and Mussolini stayed in the Villa Feltrinelli to the north of town for the last few months of his Salò Republic. Every September, the crowds pour in for Centomiglia Regatta, an international sailing race *(see p39)*. ◈ Tourist Office: Piazza Boldini 2 • Map R3 • 0365 791 243

Salò

Salò is a lovely place, a bustling workaday town in a beautiful location on the western shore of the lake. The streets leading back from the broad waterfront are good for shopping and the Renaissance Duomo rewards a brief visit. Elegant old *palazzi* line the streets, while a multitude of sleek yachts bob in the large marina. Salò famously gave its name to Mussolini's Repubblica di Salò, a puppet regime established for his last 18 months in power.
◈ Tourist Office: Piazza San Antonio 4 • Map Q4 • 0365 214 23 • www.rivieradeilimoni.it

Bagolino

A hamlet tucked away in the mountains above the western shore of Lago d'Idro, Bagolino is a world away from the refined Liberty villas of the lake below. Medieval houses tumble over each other on the steep narrow lanes, bits of frescoes remain on some of the

Arena, Verona

more noble buildings and the church has porticoed views. It is a good base for trekking in summer and skiing in winter but most people visit for the Lenten Carnival when dancers and musicians in traditional costumes and masks take to the ancient streets.
◈ Map Q2 • www.bagolinoweb.it

Limone sul Garda
Until the 1930s, Limone, set on a narrow strip of land at the northwestern end of the lake, was only reachable by boat. It survived on fishing, olive and citrus fruit production. There is one *lemonaia* (lemon frame) left in the town as a reminder of its livelihood through the centuries.
◈ Tourist Office: Via 4 Novembre, 29 • Map S2 • 0365 918987 • www. visitlimonesulgarda.com

Limone sul Garda

Malcesine
Malcesine, on the eastern shore of Lake Garda, has an appealing knot of cobbled lanes, a little harbour, a castle and the natural playground that is Monte Baldo above. In high season, the narrow streets are packed with visitors exploring the 13th-century Castello Scaligera (where Goethe was imprisoned for spying in 1786) or queueing to take the state-of-the-art cable car up Monte Baldo *(see p50)* for magnificent views of the lake.
◈ Tourist Office: Via Capitanato 6 • Map S3 • 045 740 0837 • www.malcesinepiu.it

A Day Trip from Salò to Riva

Morning

Salò is a good base for visiting the different sections of Lake Garda. Leave the comfortable lakeside town on the 11:30am fast boat service to **Riva del Garda** *(see p85)*. There will be a supplement to the normal return ferry price, available at the landing stage. The boat will pull in at the neighbouring town of Gardone for views of more Liberty villas and Grand Hotels. The following stop won't be for over half an hour as you cruise up the lake to the more rugged terrain where the mountains drop steeply down to the water. From your vantage point on board, check out pretty but crowded Malcesine on the eastern shore, and then the popular resort of Limone back on the west. Hop off the boat at Riva and explore the town centre, comparing the Teutonic touches to the distinctly more "Italian" atmosphere you left further down the lake. **Il Gallo** *(see p91)* in the shaded porticoes just back from the main waterfront square is a good choice for lunch.

Afternoon

After lunch, wander around the grounds of the Rocca or visit the Museo Civico inside the building. You can also head west through the gardens to the beaches for a dip in the cool waters of the lake. The return boat leaves at 4:15pm to whisk you back to Salò along the same route, leaving you with just about enough energy to explore the rest of the lake the next day.

Around the Region – Lake Garda and Around

Left **Castle, Arco** Centre **Cafés and restaurants in Verona** Right **Entrance to Gardaland**

TOP 10 Best of the Rest

1 Arco
Just 5 km (3 miles) north of Riva, the winter resort of Arco is topped by a 12th-century castle. It is also the centre of rock climbing for the area. *Tourist Office: Viale Palme 1 • Map S2 • 0464 532 255 • www.gardatrentino.it*

2 Torri del Benaco
This delightful resort remains one of the least spoiled on the lake. The Castello Scaligero here holds a *limonaia* (glass house for growing citrus fruits) and a museum. *Tourist Office: Viale Fratelli Lavanda 3; 045 722 5120; Museum: Open Jun–Sep: 9:30am–1pm & 4:30–7:30pm; Nov–May: Sat & Sun 9:30am–2:30pm & Oct: 9:30am–12:30pm & 2:30–6pm • Adm*

3 Bardolino
Attractive Bardolino is the place to stock up on local wine and the region's excellent olive oil. *Tourist Office: Piazzale Aldo Moro, Bardolino • Map R5 • 045 721 0078*

4 The Liston, Verona
The pink marble pavement of the Piazza Bra is lined with cafés, restaurants and *gelateries* with views of the Arena. *Map H4*

5 Desenzano
The lake's main town, Desenzano has the most buzzing nightlife around Lake Garda in the summer *(see p29).*

6 The Valvestino
This mountainous area lying between Lake Garda and Lake Idro, was border territory marking the frontier with the Austro-Hungarian empire until 1915. *Map Q3 • www.rivieradeilimoni.it*

7 Lake Ledro
Surrounded by mountains, little Lake Ledro is the highest of the northern Italian pre-Alpine lakes. The area is perfect for exploring by bike or on foot. *Map R2 • www.lagodiledro.it*

8 Punta San Vigilio
A dreamy little spot with a cypress-lined path, an attractive pay beach and an exclusive hotel where Winston Churchill came to rest at the end of World War II *(see p46).*

9 Casa di Giulietta, Verona
Seemingly a must for all visitors to Verona, this homage to Shakespeare – or to love – is in fact an invention of the 1930s. If you come though, join the crowds and stick your love note on any spare bit of wall *(see p20).*

10 Gardaland
This is Italy's premier theme park with a range of rides and activities for all the family. Avoiding the crowds can be tricky *(see p50).*

Students and over-60s frequently have discounted entry to sights.

Left **Garden in Il Vittoriale** Centre **Giardino Giusti** Right **Bamboo forest in the Heller Garden**

🔟 Garda's Parks and Gardens

1 Heller Garden, Gardone
Established in 1901 by Arturo Hruska, this oasis of bamboo forest, magnolias, Japanese water features, ferns, edelweiss and much more is now owned by the artist André Heller, who has added contemporary sculptures by the likes of Roy Lichtenstein and Keith Haring (see p49).

2 Aqua Paradise Park, Garda
A world of splashing and sliding, rapids and rides meets visitors to this extensive water-park at the south-eastern end of the lake (see p50).

3 Public Garden, Arco
Opposite the casino in the heart of Arco is a beautiful public garden filled with exotic plants and varieties of palms, and Mediterranean colours and scents. ◈ Viale delle Palme • Map S2

4 Sigurta Giardino, Valeggio sul Mincio, Verona
This park of mature trees and lawns is landscaped with a huge variety of flowers and shrubs.
◈ Via Cavour 1, Valeggio Sul Mincio • Map R6 • 045 637 1033 • Open Mar–Nov 9am–6pm • Adm • www.sigurta.it

5 Parco Baia delle Sirene, Punta San Vigilio
The Siren's Bay on Punta San Vigilio is in essence a pay beach, but it is a lovely spot set among olive groves and lawns with a sheltered bay looking across to the mountains (see p46).

6 Il Vittoriale, Gardone Riviera
The eccentric war-mongering imagination of D'Annunzio (see p90) characterizes the extensive grounds around his residence.
◈ Il Vittoriale • Map Q4 • 0365 296 511 • Open Apr–Sep: Tue–Sun 9:30am–7pm, Oct–Mar: Tue–Sun 9am–1pm • Adm

7 Isola Garda
The lake's largest island, Isola di Garda has beautifully kept grounds with English and Italian formal gardens around the 20th-century Neo-Venetian-Gothic villa.
◈ Map Q4 • 328 384 9226 • Open May–Oct • Adm • www.isoladelgarda.com

8 Parco Grotta Cascata Varone, North of Riva
A series of walkways suspend you over the spectacular gorge with white water thundering all around. ◈ Via Cascata 12, Tenno, Riva del Garda • Map S2 • 0464 521 421 • Open Sun & hol 10am–5pm Jan, Feb, Nov, Dec; closes Mar–Oct 5pm, Apr–Sep 6pm, May–Aug 7pm • Adm • www.cascata-varone.com

9 Giardino Giusti, Verona
The Giardino Giusti was laid out in the 15th century as formal gardens with fountains, grottoes and shady bowers. ◈ Map H4 • Open daily Apr–Sep: 9am–8pm, Oct–Mar: 9am–5pm • Adm • www.tourism.verona.it

10 Olive Groves, Sirmione
Stop for a break among the olive groves that line the route to the Grotte di Catullo (see p28).

Left **Il Vittoriale, Gardone Riviera** Center **Castello Scaligero** Right **Casa Mazzanti**

TOP 10 Buildings

1 San Francesco
Built in 1289, Gargnano's main church, San Francesco, retains frescoes of the same period as well as a 14th-century cloister with carved capitols.
🔊 *Via Roma, Gargnano • Map R3*

2 Casa Mazzanti
Casa Mazzanti, at the northwest end of Piazza delle Erbe in Verona, was begun in the 14th century by the della Scala family. It is one of the few surviving frescoed houses here.
🔊 *Piazza delle Erbe, Verona • Map H4*

3 Grand Hotel
Opened in 1884, this attractive Belle Epoque hotel on the Gardone Riviera offers lake-facing rooms with balconies, terraces and sweeping gardens.
🔊 *Via Zanardelli 84, Gardone Riviera • Map Q4 • 0365 20 261*

4 Palazzo Pretorio
This 14th-century *palazzo* built by the della Scala family stands on Riva's lakeside square, Piazza III Novembre, surrounded by stone porticos. 🔊 *Piazza 3 Novembre, Riva del Garda • Map S2*

5 Palazzo Maffei
The three-tiered Baroque Palazzo Maffei stands at one end of the central Veronese square – Piazza delle Erbe. It is crowned by four statues of Roman gods and goddesses and one of Hercules. 🔊 *Piazza delle Erbe, Verona • Map H4*

6 Rocca Scaligera
Constructed by Mastino I della Scala from Verona in the 13th century, Sirmione's moated castle guards the entrance to the village *(see p29)*.

7 Castello Scaligero, Torri del Benaco
The western tower in Torri del Benaco's castle is a remnant of the original Roman fortification; other sections are from the Veronese strengthening in 1383. Drop by the *limonaia (see p88)*.
🔊 *2, Viale Fratelli Lavanda, Torri del Benaco • Map R4 • 045 629 6111 • www.museodelcastelloditorridelbenaco.it*

8 Il Vittoriale
This extraordinary complex of museums, gardens and villa in Gardone is the ex-residence and monument to the Fascist author Gabriele d'Annunzio *(see p89)*.
🔊 *www.vittoriale.it*

9 The Arena
Verona's Roman amphitheatre has a seating capacity of 15,000 spectators and is the venue for pop and jazz concerts as well as summer opera extravaganzas *(see p21)*.

10 Castello Scaligero, Malcesine
Originally constructed by Lombards, the Veronese della Scala family further fortified Malcesine's castle *(see p87)*.
🔊 *Via Castello, Malcesine • Map S3 • 045 657 0333*

Price Categories

For a three-course meal for one, with half a bottle of wine (or equivalent meal), taxes, and extra charges.	€ under €30
	€€ €30–€40
	€€€ €40–€50
	€€€€ €50–€60
	€€€€€ over €60

Above **Traditional wine bar, Bottega del Vino**

ⓒ10 Places to Eat

1 Antica Locanda Mincio
This ancient inn by the Ponte Visconteo appropriately serves a mix of Mantovan and Veronese cooking, including the *tortelli* that Valeggio is famed for.
⊗ *Borgetto 12, Via Buonarroti, Valeggio sul Mincio • Map R6 • 045 795 0059 • Closed Wed & Thu • €€*

2 Osteria il Gallo
This small restaurant under the stone arches in the central Riva serves hearty mountain dishes including dumplings and stews with good Trento wines. ⊗ *Piazza San Rocco 12, Riva del Garda • Map S2 • 0464 556 200 • Closed Nov–Feb D • €*

3 La Rucola
This rustic-chic restaurant near the castle has top-notch food. The menu offers lake-fish and meat dishes but also includes crispy wood-fired-oven pizzas.
⊗ *Via Strentelle 7, Sirmione • Map R5 • 030 916 326 • Closed Thu • €€€€*

4 Antica Trattoria alle Rose
Excellent home-style cooking using freshly caught fish or locally sourced ingredients.
⊗ *Via Gasparo da Salò 33, Salò • Map Q4 • 0365 43220 • Close Wed • €€€*

5 Cavallino
Sardinian cooking mixed with the best of Garda cuisine creates this gourmet experience in a back street away from the castle. ⊗ *Via Murachette 29, Desenzano • Map Q5 • 030 912 0217 • Closed Sun D, Mon & Nov–mid-Dec • €€€€€*

6 Ristorante 100 km
This stylish restaurant in the Hotel Bellerive *(see p113)* serves produce sourced from within 100 km (62 miles) of Salò; the quality fare is mainly inspired by Brescian and lake-based recipes. ⊗ *Hotel Bellerive, Via Pietro da Salò, Salò • Map Q4 • 0365 520 410 • Closed Dec & Jan • €€€€*

7 Villa Fiordaliso
The Liberty dining rooms of this Grand Hotel on the lakeside in Gardone set the scene for an haute-cuisine feast.
⊗ *Corso Zanardelli 132, Gardone Riviera • Map Q4 • 0365 20 158 • Closed Mon, Tue L, Oct–Mar • €€€€€*

8 Restel de Ferr
Game and fish top the bill of fare at this family-run restaurant with a garden just outside Riva. Homemade bread and home-grown vegetables are served with Lombard and Trento touches. ⊗ *Via Restel de Fer 10, Riva • Map S2 • 0464 553 481 • Closed Wed (winter) • €€€*

9 Gardesana
This atmospheric hotel-restaurant serves good food with lots of local fish and regional wines. ⊗ *Piazza Calderini 5, Torri del Benaco • Map R4 • 045 722 5411 • Closed Nov–mid-Mar • €€€*

10 Bottega del Vino
Wine-based dishes are served in this wine bar that has elegant rooms displaying special vintages.
⊗ *Via Scudo di Francia 3a, Verona • Map H4 • 045 800 4535 • Closed Tue • €€€*

➤ *Recommend your favourite restaurant on* **traveldk.com**

Left **Certosa di Pavia** Centre **Palazzo Te, Mantova** Right **Statue at Castello Sforzesco, Milan**

Milan and Southern Lombardy

Milan surprises visitors with a rich fabric of historical treasures juxtaposed with its current incarnation as a fashion centre. Outside the city, the flat agricultural lands defined by the River Po and its irrigation canals are peppered with ancient hamlets, monasteries and farmsteads. Several towns

stretch across the plains with a life of their own and a cultural heritage second to none. The Carthusian monastery just outside the town is the apex of Pavia's monuments, while Cremona lives off its 17th-century fame as a centre for violin-making and has an attractive Romanesque cathedral. But Mantova is the most impressive of the three, with much remaining from when the town was a centre of Renaissance art and architecture during the 14th to 17th centuries under the rule of the Gonzaga family.

Boutique in the Navigli District, Milan

🔟 Sights

1. The Duomo, Milan
2. *The Last Supper*, Milan
3. Pinacoteca di Brera, Milan
4. Castello Sforzesco, Milan
5. Navigli District, Milan
6. Pinacoteca Ambrosiana, Milan
7. Triennale, Milan
8. The Torrazzo, Cremona
9. Certosa di Pavia, Pavia
10. Palazzo Te, Mantova

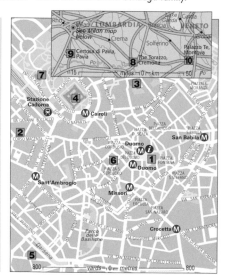

For more information see www.milanoinfotourist.com, www.aptcremona.it and www.turismo.mantova.it

Detail of the Duomo exterior, Milan

The Duomo, Milan
Milan's monumental cathedral presides over the central Piazza del Duomo, a huge square lined with stately porticoes. The piazza was created by clearing medieval streets and buildings in the 19th century to provide a better view of the church. To this day, the Duomo remains the city's social and geographical hub. The exterior is a confection of lofty pinnacles, statuary and filigree marble work. No visit to Milan is complete without a trip to the roof to clamber among the spires and buttresses and marvel at the view *(see pp18–19)*.

The Last Supper, Milan
Leonardo da Vinci finished painting *The Last Supper* on the refectory wall of the Dominican monastery in 1498. The work is outstanding for its portrayal of the disciples' emotions at the moment when Christ announces he will be betrayed. The restricted visits and filtered air create a rarefied atmosphere for a masterpiece that has survived against the odds. Using oil paint rather than watercolours meant the painting began to disintegrate almost immediately. To add to the damage, Napoleon's troops used the wall for target practice and Allied bombs destroyed the rest of the complex, leaving just this wall standing in 1943 *(see p17)*.

Pinacoteca di Brera, Milan
Napoleon opened this public gallery in 1805 to display works of art requisitioned from churches, monasteries and aristocrats throughout the north of Italy. Works include Mantegna's haunting *The Dead Christ*, Piero della Francesco's stylized *Madonna with Child, Angels, Saints and Federico da Montefeltro,* and Caravaggio's touchingly realistic *Supper at Emmaus*. An enjoyable and well organized museum with a good audio guide *(see p16)*.

Castello Sforzesco, Milan
The rulers of Milan, the Visconti, began construction of this castle in 1368, but it was under Ludovico Sforza that it became the centre of Milan's Renaissance court, employing artists such as Da Vinci and Bramante. These days the castle's museums are the main draw, with a wealth of art taken from Lombardy's churches by Napoleon's troops, furniture, and Michelangelo's touching, unfinished *Pietà (see p17)*.

Façade of the Castello Sforzesco

Rice

Rice was introduced to Italy in the Middle Ages from the Far East. Southern Lombardy's flat plains and climate proved ideal for rice cultivation with their sunny summers and plentiful water. It is found on the plates of all Italian homes in the form of risotto.

5 Navigli District, Milan

The mighty Naviglio Grande and the Naviglio Pavese lead off from the Darsena, or basin, down to the River Po and so to the Adriatic Sea. The canalside area was a working neighbourhood with tenement housing – *case ringhiera* – warehouses and factories. Since the canals fell out of use in the 1970s, the area has gradually become a focus for the city's nightlife with bars and restaurants lining the waterways. It is also something of an artists' corner with crafts workshops and galleries situated in the old courtyards (see p17).

6 Pinacoteca Ambrosiana, Milan

This gallery was founded by Cardinal Federico Borromeo in 1621 under the zealous atmosphere of the Counter Reformation and was conceived to help educate the public of their Catholic heritage. The collection includes important works of art, quirky curios and a priceless

The Torazzo, Cremona

library of manuscripts. Some of the prize exhibits were collected by the Cardinal himself – a preparatory cartoon by Raffaello and Leonardo da Vinci's *Codex Atlanticus* – others were added later. ◎ *Piazza Pio 2, Milan • Map V4 • 02 806 921 • Open Tue–Sun 9am–7pm • Adm • www.ambrosiana.it*

7 Triennale, Milan

Giovanni Muzzio's exhibition space, based in the Palazzo dell'Arte (1931), provides a focus for the city's contemporary design and architecture activities. Built as home to the tri-annual design exhibition, it now offers a selection of permanent and temporary exhibitions, a reference library, a specialist bookshop, a great café-restaurant (see p98) and a buzzing bar outside in the summer. ◎ *Viale Alemagna 6, Milan • Map T2 • 02 724 341 • Open Tue–Sun 10:30am–8.30pm, closes 11pm Thu & Fri • Adm • www.triennale.it*

8 The Torrazzo, Cremona

At 112-m (413-ft) high, the Torrazzo, rising out of Cremona's Piazza del Comune, is the tallest bell tower in Europe. The 502 steps to the top lead to wonderful views over the Po plain. The tower dates from the mid-13th century

Shops and cafés in the Navigli District, Milan

and is topped with a Gothic *ghirlanda* (spire). ◎ *Piazza del Comune • Map E6 • 0372 27386 • Open Tue–Sun 10am–1pm & 2:30–6pm*

Certosa di Pavia, Pavia

This charterhouse complex, founded in 1396 as a mausoleum for the Visconti family, is worth visiting not just for its splendid architecture but also for the insight into the daily lives of this meditative order. A compulsory guided tour takes you through the tombs and artwork and out to the closed areas of the monastery. ◎ *Via del Monumento, Pavia • Map C5 • Open Nov–Feb: 9–11am & 2:30–4:30pm; Mar–Oct: 9–11:30am & 2:30–5pm; Apr–Sep: 2:30–5:30pm; May–Aug: 2:30–6pm • Tip welcomed • www. certosadipavia.com*

Lofty arches of the Palazzo Te, Mantova

Palazzo Te, Mantova

On the southern edge of the town centre, the Palazzo Te was built as a summer retreat for Federico II Gonzaga and a residence for his mistress. Begun in 1525, the Mannerist palace and gardens are a creation by Giulio Romano, inspired by the villas of ancient Rome. In the palace rooms, the stuccoed walls and ceilings create a world of their own. ◎ *Viale Te, Mantova • Map H4 • 0376 323 266 • Open Mon 1–6pm Tue–Sun 9am–6pm • Adm • www.palazzote.it*

A Day Exploring Milan's Churches

Morning

🕐 Start the day with Da Vinci's **The Last Supper** *(see p93)*. Book your slot a couple of months in advance. Then drop by the neighbouring church, Santa Maria delle Grazie, with its giant dome and charming courtyard by Bramante. Cross Corso Magenta and head down to Sant'Ambrogio, the 12th-century church founded by and housing the remains of the city's patron saint, Saint Ambrose. From here dodge round the back of the church and through ancient residential streets to Largo Carrobbio, from where you can visit the San Lorenzo alle Colonne, reputedly Leonardo da Vinci's favourite Milanese church. Then, follow the Corso south through the medieval arch down to Sant'Eustorgio. This one holds the bones of the Magi and the Renaissance Portinari Chapel, accessed to the left of the church entrance. For lunch, head round the back of the church and across Parco delle Vetra to **Cantina della Vetra** *(see p99)*.

Afternoon

After lunch, either walk along Via Torino or hop on to a tram heading to the **Duomo** *(see p93)*. Buy a ticket from a newspaper stand before boarding and stamp it in the orange box. After exploring the inside of the Duomo, head up to the roof for a close-up of the marble work and to take in the unbeatable views across the city and – on a clear day – over to the Alps.

Around the Region – Milan and Southern Lombardy

Left **La Scala, Milan** Centre **Lush grounds of the Parco Sempione** Right **Sant'Ambrogio, Milan**

Best of the Rest

1 Parco Sempione
Milan's most popular park is home to the Torre Branca and is scattered with cafés and an aquarium. ❧ *Milan • Map X2 • Torre Branca: Open (winter) Wed, Sat & Sun 10:30am; closes Wed 6:30pm, Sat midnight, Sun 7pm; open (summer) Tue–Sun 9:30pm–12am; closes Fri 6pm, Sat & Sun 7:30pm • Adm • www.branca.it*

2 Museo Bagatti Valsecchi
This museum houses the Bagatti Valsecchi brothers' collection of 16th-century carvings, frescoes, tapestries and furniture. ❧ *Via Santo Spirito 10/ Via Gesù 5, Milan • Map X3 • Open Tue–Sun 1–5:45pm • Adm • www.museobagattivalsecchi.org*

3 Museo Poldi Pezzoli
Gian Giacomo Poldi Pezzoli's vast collection of armoury, porcelain, jewellery, tapestries and paintings are all displayed in his house. ❧ *Via Manzoni 12, Milan • Map W3 • Open 10am–6pm Wed–Mon • Adm*

4 Sant'Ambrogio
This 12th-century church is Milan's most important building as it houses the remains of the city's patron saint *(see p17)*. ❧ *Map U4*

5 San Fedele
Begun in 1569 by Pelligrini, San Fedele in Milan is the most celebrated example of Counter-Reformation architecture. ❧ *Map W3 • Open daily 7am–2:30pm & 4–7pm*

6 La Scala
Milan's internationally renowned opera house hosts the world's top performers *(see p16)*.

7 Museo Stradivariano and Sala dei Violini
The museum displays Stradivarius' instrument models and tools and in the Sala dei Violini, million-dollar instruments are played. ❧ *Museo: Via Ugolani Dati, Cremona; Sala dei Violini, Palazzo del Comune • Map E6 • Open 9am–6pm Tue–Sat, 10am–6pm Sun; Sala dei Violini: open Apr–Jun & Sep: Mon • Adm*

8 The Duomo
The Romanesque Duomo in Cremona has a splendid façade with a huge rose window. ❧ *Piazza del Duomo, Cremona • Map E6 • Open Mon–Sat 10:30am–noon & 3:30–6pm, Sun 12–12:30pm & 3:30–5:30pm*

9 Palazzo Ducale
This *palazzo* is the heart of the Renaissance court of Ludovico II Gonzago. ❧ *Piazza Sordello 40, Mantova • Map H6 • Open Tue–Sun 8:15am–7:15pm • Adm • www.mantovaducale.it*

10 San Lorenzo alle Colonne
This ancient church has an octagonal plan, well lit by the windows. ❧ *Corso di Porta Ticinese 39, Milan • Map V5 • Open daily 7:30am–12:30pm & 2:30–6:45pm*

Left **Boutique in Galleria Vittoria Emanuele II** Centre **Boutique, Corsa di Porta Ticinese** Right **Olives**

🔟 Shopping in Milan

1 Galleria Vittorio Emanuele II

This lofty 19th-century mall offers a mixture of cafés, elegant old boutiques and expensive tourist paraphernalia *(see p17)*. ✎ *Map W3*

2 Quadrilatero d'Oro

Exquisite boutiques from the world's top fashion houses lead off the pedestrianized lanes *(see p17)*. ✎ *Map X2*

3 Rinascente

Milan's main department store is a visitor's delight. Bite-sized selections in all departments offer the best of Italian and international goods. Try the food hall upstairs. ✎ *Piazza Duomo • Map W4 • Open Mon–Thu 9:30am–9pm, Sun 10am–9pm, Fri & Sat closes 10pm*

4 Brera and Moscova

Wandering around the neighbourhoods of Brera and Moscova, you will discover specialist shops, stylish boutiques and gourmet delicatessens on every corner. ✎ *Map V2*

5 Mercato Wagner and Street Markets

Daily street markets are a feast of fresh produce; the tourist offices have addresses. Alternatively, Mercato Wagner offers the same cornucopia of fruit, vegetables, cheeses and cold meats under one colourful roof. ✎ *Map N6 • Open Tue–Sat 8:30am–1pm & 4–7:30pm, Mon mornings only*

6 Outlets

Milan and the surrounding countryside are dotted with outlets and factory shops. From genuine designer labels to discount knitwear, bargains are available. ✎ *Il Salvagente, Via Bronzetti 16 • Open Mon 3–7pm & Tue 10am–7pm*

7 Corso di Porta Ticinese

In recent years the Corso di Porta Ticinese has established itself as the heart of alternative and trend fashion in Milan. Italian and international firms jostle for position along the ancient street.

8 Spazio Armani

A chic mall dedicated to different Giorgio Armani ranges, from mens- and womenswear to housewares and furnishings. There is also a slick café, Japanese restaurant and chocolate counter. ✎ *Via Manzoni 31 • Map W2*

9 Furniture and Design

Milan's furniture and design showrooms pepper the streets leading off San Babila. While Via Durini and Corso Europa are best for contemporary furniture and design classics, Corso Monforte has a host of lighting specialists. ✎ *Around San Babila • Map X3*

10 Antiques Fairs

The last Sunday in the month sees the canalside lined with the Mercatone del Naviglio Grande. Via Fiori Chiari in Brera hosts a fair for smaller antiques on the third Saturday of the month. ✎ *Map V2*

Around the Region – Milan and Southern Lombardy

Left **Façade of Le Biciclette** Centre *Pasticceria* **in the Cova** Right **Chic decor of Design Café**

Cafés and Bars

1 Le Biciclette
The definitive *aperitivo* bar off a leafy street near the Porta di Ticenese. A designer crowd of 30-somethings keep the place lively well after the zinc bar has been cleared of nibbles. ✎ *Conca del Naviglio 10, Milan • Map C4*

2 Zucca
Sip an *aperitivo* while taking in the lovely Art Deco mosaics at one of Milan's most famous bars. Opt for a house Campari, invented here in the 1860s. ✎ *Galleria Vittorio Emanuelle II 21, Piazza del Duomo, Milan • Map W3 • Closed Mon*

3 Cova
This tea room and *pasticceria* (pastry shop) has been run by the same family since 1817. The chocolates are exquisite as is the Christmas *panettone* (candied-peel bread). ✎ *Via Montenapoleone 8, Milan • Map X3 • 02 7600 5599*

4 Chocolat
A modern coffee bar round the corner from *The Last Supper*, offering a selection of home-made ice creams. In winter, the hot chocolate is divine. ✎ *Via Boccaccio 9, Milan • Map U3*

5 Portici del Comune
The outdoor tables at this bar offer unbeatable views of the façade of the Duomo and the central piazza of Cremona. The coffee is among the best served in town. ✎ *Piazza del Comune 2, Cremona • Map E6 • Closed Tue (winter)*

6 Bar Bianco
This unassuming park café serves panini, coffee and cool drinks during the day, but on summer evenings it transforms into one of the hotspots in town. ✎ *Parco Sempione, Milan • Map U1*

7 Luini
A great little spot, steps away from the Duomo, serving *panzerotti* (deep-fried mini calzone) – tomato and mozzarella fillings are the most traditional – to the queuing crowd. Standing room only. ✎ *Via Radegonda 16, Milan • Map T2 • Closed Sun • 0286 461917*

8 Design Café
A slick café-restaurant, with designer chairs, stylish clientele and a huge picture window over-looking Parco Sempione. ✎ *La Triennale, Viale Alemagna, Milan • Map T2 • Closed Mon*

9 Bar Radetzy
This stylish bar in the hip Moscova neighbourhood is a good pit stop at any time. Beat regulars to the couple of tables on the pavement outside and watch Milan go by. ✎ *Largo La Foppa 5, Milan • Map V1*

10 Buca del Gabbia
A snug little wine bar just round the corner from Piazza Sordello in Mantova makes the perfect spot to settle down for a glass of wine or an after-dinner drink. ✎ *Via Cavour 98, Mantova • Map H6 • Closed Mon*

To save a little cash, remember that a drink at the bar will be much cheaper than one sitting down.

Price Categories

For a three-course meal for one, with half a bottle of wine (or equivalent meal), taxes, and extra charges.

€	under €30
€€	€30–€40
€€€	€40–€50
€€€€	€50–€60
€€€€€	over €60

Left **Ochina Bianca** Right **Diners at Masuelli San Marco**

Restaurants

Masuelli San Marco
For authentic Milanese food and atmosphere this is the best choice, just a taxi ride from the city centre. The menu includes tripe, rice and meat dishes. ✆ *Viale Umbria 80, Milan • Map C4 • 02 5518 4138 • Closed Sun, Mon L & Aug • €€€€*

Ristorante Cracco
The two Michelin-starred chef Carlo Cracco has broken away from his association with the Peck delicatessen empire but continues to produce some of the city's best Milanese dishes with a twist. ✆ *Via Victor Hugo 4, Milan • Map W3 • 02876 764 • Closed Sat lunch & Sun • €€€€€*

Il Cigno
This elegant restaurant occupies a 16th-century *palazzo* with a little garden, and serves seasonal specialities. ✆ *Piazza d'Arco 1, Mantova • Map H6 • 0376 327 101 • Closed Mon, Tue & Aug • €€€€*

Cantina della Vetra
Gnocchi fritti (fried potato balls) are the house speciality at this bustling trattoria with friendly service. ✆ *Via Pio IV, Milan • Map V5 • Closed Sat lunch & Sun eve • €€*

Ochina Bianca
Excellent Mantovan dishes are served in this simple trattoria with a limited menu using quality ingredients. Part of the Slow Food movement. ✆ *Via G, Finzi 2, Mantova • Map H6 • 0376 323700 • Closed Mon • €€*

Joia
A gourmet heaven: enjoy the award-winning cuisine in the contemporary dining room. Mainly vegetarian with a few fish dishes; emphasis is on discovery and harmony. ✆ *Via Panfilo Castaldi 18, Milan • Map Y1 • 02 2952 2124 • €€€€€*

La Sosta
Fine seasonal cooking includes the winter speciality of *bollito* (meat and vegetables boiled in broth) served with gem-coloured *mostarda di Cremona*. ✆ *Via Sicardo 9, Cremona • Map E6 • 0372 456 656 • Closed Sun eve & Mon • €€*

Trattoria Milanese
Located at the heart of town, this elegant restaurant serves up hearty Milanese staples. Try their creamy *risotto alla Milanese*. ✆ *Via Santa Marta 11, Milan • Map V4 • 02 8645 1991 • Closed Tue • €€*

Anema e Cozze
Located just by the canal, this bright, breezy Neopolitan restaurant serves tasty seafood, fine salads and authentic pizzas. ✆ *Via Casale 7, Milan • Map T6 • 02 837 5459 • €*

Ponte Rosso
Carefully prepared dishes are served in this bustling canalside location. Alongside Lombard specialities, wider Italian influences offer an alternative. ✆ *Ripa di Porte Ticinese 23, Milan • Map C4 • 02 837 3132• Closed Sun & Mon lunch • €€*

STREETSMART

Planning Your Trip
102

Getting To and Around
103

Useful Information
104

Special Interest
Holidays
105

Banking and
Communications
106

Security and Health
107

Things to Avoid
108

Budget Tips
109

Dining Tips
110

Accommodation Tips
111

Places to Stay
112–117

ITALIAN LAKES' TOP 10

Left **Currency** Right **Clock at a railway station**

🔟 Planning Your Trip

1 What to Pack
Italians dress smartly; in the larger towns you may feel out of place if you dress too informally. A tie, however, will not be needed, although a suitable jacket would rarely be inappropriate. You will need to cover your shoulders and wear over-knee-length shorts or skirts while visiting churches and other religious sites.

2 Currency
The currency in Italy is the euro (€), which is divided into one hundred cents. The currency in Switzerland is the Swiss Franc (Fr. or CHF), which is also divided into cents. Most establishments in Switzerland, however, including shops, restaurants, hotels and ferry companies will readily accept euros for transactions.

3 Passports and Visas
Citizens of the European Union (EU), the USA, Canada, New Zealand and Australia can enter Italy and Switzerland with just a valid passport and stay for 90 days. If you wish to extend your stay, you should check with your consulate for further information.

4 Making Reservations
Not booking ahead could leave you out in the cold at certain times of year. A slot to see Da Vinci's *The Last Supper* needs to be booked at least a month ahead, and more for weekends and in the summer. August is a very busy month on the lakes and an advance reservation will ensure you get the bed of your choice. Similarly, book ahead in Milan during the fashion shows (last week of Feb and Sep) or during the Design and Furniture Fair (mid-Apr).

5 Insurance
As with any trip, it is advisable to make sure that all your belongings are covered by travel insurance, and that health emergencies will be taken care of by local services or your health insurance. Also confirm that the pre-article limit covers your most valuable items, and that "dangerous sports" (such as hiking and watersports) are included in the insurance.

6 Driving Licence
Non-EU licence holders need a valid driving licence and an international driving permit as do holders of UK pre-1991 driving licences. Other EU drivers simply need to carry their photocard licence.

7 Time Difference
Italy is on Central European Time (CET): one hour ahead of London, six hours ahead of New York and eight hours behind Sydney.

8 Electrical Appliances
The electrical supply in Italy is 220V, although appliances requiring 240V will also work. Plugs are generally two pin but the diameter of the pins in some older establishments may differ, so a multi-plug adapter is very useful. Electrical equipment from the UK will need an adapter as will appliances from the US, which require a 220-to-110 transformer.

9 Baby's Needs
Nappies and milk formula are significantly more expensive in Italy than in other European countries, and baby foods tend to have more sugar and salt added. Health food shops in the larger towns can be a source of alternative brands.

10 Membership Cards
Members of the National Trust or the Royal Horticultural Society should bring their membership cards along as it allows free or discounted entry fees to various properties on the lakes. Similarly, an international student card, or even a university or college card, will help with various discounts around the region.

Left **Ferry in the lakes region** Centre **A local bus** Right **Train at Central Station, Milan**

🔟 Getting To and Around

1 Airports
Malpensa, to the northwest of Milan, is the region's intercontinental hub; Linate to the east is the city's second airport serving mainly international flights. Airports at Bergamo, Brescia, Verona and Lugano (Switzerland) are well linked to the towns and villages of the lakes region. ⊗ *Milan Malpensa & Linate: www.sea-aeroportimilano.it; Bergamo: www.sacbo.it; Brescia: www.aeroportobrescia.it; Verona: www.aeroportoverona.it; Lugano: www.lugano-airport.ch*

2 Driving to Italy
The route over the Alps from France or Switzerland is a spectacular entry into Italy. Note that French and Italian motorways all charge tolls, which are not expensive but they add up. In Switzerland, you must buy a windowscreen vignette (€25) from customs officers or petrol stations.

3 Trains to Italy
Travelling with Eurostar and the French high-speed TGV to Milan takes around 11 hours from London and involves a change of stations in Paris. It is an enjoyable trip, although most of the journey is at night and prices are not competitive compared to air travel. ⊗ *0870 0518 6186 • www.eurostar.com*

4 Coaches to Italy
Buses leave from London for Milan several times a week and less frequently to Brescia, Turin and Verona. The journey takes 23 hours and is unlikely to be cheaper than a no-frills flight. ⊗ *08705 143 219; • www.eurolines.co.uk*

5 Getting Around by Ferry
Simple and efficient, the lake ferries are also good value and the perfect alternative to traffic-jammed roads. The main lakes also have car ferries crossing the middle. ⊗ *Lake Lugano: www.lakelugano.ch • Lakes Maggiore, Como & Garda: www.navigazionelaghi.it • Lake Iseo: www.navigazionelagoiseo.it*

6 Getting Around by Train
The national train service is good value and efficient but it does not serve the lakes well. It does, however, connect all the main towns with a mixture of express trains and local stoppers. ⊗ *06 44101 • www.trenitalia.com*

7 Getting Around by Bus
Local buses link the lakeside villages with a regular, if not frequent, service; tickets are generally sold on the bus. The tickets for urban bus services usually need to be bought from newspaper kiosks or bars before boarding. Milan, Bergamo and southern Lake Garda have open-topped tourist buses that offer a hop-on-hop-off service around the sights. ⊗ *www.zaniviaggi.it*

8 Rules of the Road
In Italy drive on the right and keep to the speed limits: 50 kmph in built-up areas, 110 kmph on dual carriageways and 130kph on motorways. Dip your headlights outside built-up areas and carry a warning triangle and a fluorescent jacket for breakdowns. Carry car documents (not photocopies) and your passport when driving.

9 Cycling Tips
Italy is passionate about cycling and you will see packs of multi-coloured cyclists everywhere. Most airlines will carry bikes, or they can be rented throughout the region. Flat, challenging, on-road or mountain-biking – opportunities abound *(see pp40–41).*

10 Driving in the Lakes Region
Much of the lakes region is best explored by public transport: the larger towns and the lakeside roads see heavy traffic and insufficient parking. Italian motorways are toll roads; you pay on exit with cash or a credit card. Most petrol stations close at 7pm and all day Sunday.

Left **Tourist office sign** Right **Newspaper stall at a railway station**

TOP 10 Useful Information

1 Tourist Information
Most towns and large lakeside villages have tourist offices offering anything from printed fliers to detailed walks in the area, room-booking services and guided tours. On the whole, the staff speak English.

2 State Tourist Boards
Information from the Italian tourist board is easily available and their website can give you a flavour of the region. Switzerland Tourism, however, provide details of anything and everything that you might possibly need. § www.enit.it • www.ticino.ch

3 Public Holidays
Most shops, sights and some restaurants will be closed on public holidays. Public transport will be significantly reduced and the lakes are likely to be inundated with daytrippers from surrounding towns.

4 Phone Numbers
To call Italy from abroad, dial the international access code, then 39 and then the number including the initial zero. To call Switzerland, dial the international access code, then 41 and then the number excluding the initial zero. In Italy, the area code needs to be dialled every time.

5 Media
Italian TV stations have little to offer foreigners and larger hotels usually offer CNN and BBC. However, Italian print journalism is of a higher standard and international press is always readily available.

6 Websites
Outdated information is not uncommon on Italian websites and a large number of places, including tourist offices and resorts, do not have websites at all. Italian hotels are increasingly offering online booking nowadays, but it is always wise to get a written confirmation.

7 High Season
High season around the lakes is June to September. Places are usually open from Easter to the end of October, but over the winter many of the lake villages and their hotels shut up shop.

8 Weather
It is warm to hot in summer and cold and often foggy in winter. July is the hottest month with an average of 26°C (79°F) while May, June and September are pleasant. Flash thunderstorms are common in the second half of August.

9 Maps
Most tourist offices can give you a free town plan. If you are looking for more detailed maps for striding out into the countryside, the Istituto Geografico Centrale and Kompass series are available in bookshops. The Swisstopo maps, in Switzerland, are excellent reference material.

10 Opening Hours
Shops and businesses open from 9am to 1–2pm and from 3–4pm to 6–7pm Mon–Sat; some still close on Monday mornings. Most museums are open Tue–Sat from 9–10am to 6–7pm, sometimes with a two-hour break for lunch.

Public Holidays
- *1 January: New Year's Day*
- *6 January: Epiphany*
- *Pasquetta; Easter Monday*
- *25 April: Liberation Day (not in Switzerland)*
- *1 May: Labour Day*
- *2 June: Republic Day (not in Switzerland)*
- *1 August: Swiss National Day (Switzerland only)*
- *15 August: Ferragosto; Assumption of the Blessed Virgin Mary*
- *1 November: All Souls Day*
- *8 December: Immaculate Conception of the Blessed Virgin Mary*

For timetables of public transport in Lombardy see www.trasporti.regione.lombardia.it

Left **Sailing, Lake Como** Right **Cyclists in Riva del Garda**

🔟 Special Interest Holidays

1 Sailing and Watersports

The north of Lake Garda around Torbole is the most famous destination in the region for watersports, but all the lakes have windsurfing and sailing dinghies for rent. Kite boarding and canyoning is often available too. Tourist offices have lists of the many local operators *(see p10–11 and p80)*. ⬥ *Tabo Surf Centre, Lake Como; Map P1; 0344 94062 • Pierwindsurf, Lake Garda; Map S2; 0464 550 928; www.pierwindsurf.it • Surf Segnana, Lake Garda; Map S2; 0464 505 963 • Surfcenter, Lido Blu, Lake Garda; Map S2; 0464 506 349; www.surflb.com*

2 Senior Citizens

The mild climate and the easily accessible mixture of sights have made the lakes popular with senior citizens for decades. Many holiday companies, such as Just You and Saga, arrange tours and single-base breaks in hotels with good accessibility. ⬥ *www.justyou.co.uk • www.saga.co.uk*

3 Cycling

Whether you are interested in asphalt or off-road biking, this region has much to offer. Cycles can be hired throughout the area and many airlines will allow you to bring your own. The Italian organization Italy Bike Hotels

(www.Italybikehotels.it) suggest itineraries and recommends specially equipped hotels. See also www.hookedoncycling.co.uk and www.cycleitalia.com

4 Wine-Tasting

Raise your glasses to Franciacorta's bubbly, nose a powerful Amarone or savour a Soave. Several well-organized companies arrange wine-tasting holidays often combined with other interests such as opera or walking. ⬥ *www.arblasterandclarke.com • www.italian-connection.co.uk*

5 Villas and Gardens

Visiting the lakes' historical villas and their luxurious gardens with an expert guide adds to the enjoyment of the experience. ⬥ *www.martinrandall.com • www.saga.co.uk*

6 Study Tours

Sign up for a full term or just a couple of weeks studying anything from Italian history and culture to opera singing or clothes design at various centres around the lakes ⬥ *www.ideaverona.com • www.ied.it*

7 Spectator Sports Breaks

There is no better place to enjoy Italian football than at a team's home stadium. Many companies

will organize your break including flights, accommodation and tickets. Formula 1 events outside Milan in Monza are the focus of another popular sporting break. ⬥ *www.redcardevents.co.uk • www.footballencounters.co.uk*

8 Opera Breaks

Have the hassle taken out of booking tickets at Verona's August operas in the Roman Arena and Milan's winter opera season. Opera breaks are often offered with walking or wine-tasting holidays.
⬥ www.citalia.com
• www.crystallakes.co.uk
• www.saga.co.uk

9 Walking

Whether you want a guide or to strike out on your own, the combination of mountains and lakes is almost limitless; you will be spoiled for choice. Backroads US has information on active holidays. ⬥ 800-462-2848 • www.backroads.com

10 Learning Italian

The quickest and most memorable way to learn a language is to study in the country itself. Choose a lakeside academy or study in a nearby town to perfect your pronunciation.
⬥ *For details on courses available: www.ihworld.com, www.ihworld.com, www.ilcentro.net and www.lingua.it.*

Left **Bank** Centre **Internet café** Right **Public phone**

Banking and Communications

1 Money

Italy's currency is the euro, which replaced the lira in 2002. There are seven euro notes – in denominations of 500, 200, 100, 50, 20, 10, and 5 euros – each a different colour and size. There are also eight different coin denominations – 2 and 1 euros and then 50, 20, 10, 5, 2 and 1 cents.

2 Banks

You will find at least one bank in most villages and the larger resorts and towns have several. Opening hours are usually on Monday to Friday, from 8:30am to 1:30pm and then for another hour in the afternoon, often 2:30–3:30pm. Banks offer the best rate of exchange for cash and they will almost invariably have an ATM for direct access to funds.

3 Bureaux de Change

The rates of exchange at a bureaux de change are generally significantly worse than at banks, but they are open for longer hours. In Italy, the bureaux de change on station forecourts have particularly bad rates; in Switzerland, however, they usually offer better rates than the banks.

4 Credit Cards

Credit cards *(carte)* are a useful backup source of funds and can be used in ATMs with a PIN number that has been authorized for use overseas. Note that in Italy, credit cards are not particularly widely used and many restaurants – and even some of the cheaper hotels – will only take cash.

5 Postal Services

Post offices are open from Monday to Saturday, between 8:30am and 1pm, and can be very busy during the mid-morning hours. Stamps *(francobolli)* can also be bought from most postcard shops as well as from *tabacchi* (tobacconists). Post boxes are easily identifiable by their red colour.

6 Postal Charges

The price of sending a standard letter or post-card anywhere in Europe is 65 cents. Posting the same to destinations in the USA, Australia and New Zealand costs 85 cents. Within Italy, the price for sending a standard letter or postcard is 60 cents.

7 Internet Points

Internet points are increasingly common around the region and many hotels now offer the service to their customers. Alternatively, there are a number of cafés with Wi-Fi services, or pay-as-you-use points in bars, libraries and phone centres.

8 Telephones

Coin-operated public phones are increasingly difficult to find in both Italy and Switzerland. Buy a phone card *(scheda telefonica)* from a news-paper stand or *tabacchi* and follow the English instructions. Otherwise, buy a prepaid phone card from the same places and dial the toll-free number to give your PIN (written on the back of the card). The rates are significantly cheaper for calls abroad.

9 Mobile Phones

If you plan to take your phone with you, then ensure that you have made the necessary "roaming" arrangements before leaving. Mobile phones in Italy and Switzerland work on the GSM European standard, which is compatible with UK phones and those from the rest of Europe, Australia and New Zealand, but not with most from the US and Canada.

10 Dialling Codes

The code is integral to Italian numbers and must be dialled even in the same city. To call home from Italy, dial 00 then your country code (UK: 44; Australia: 61; New Zealand: 64) and then the number excluding the initial zero. Dial 001 and then the full number for calling the US and Canada.

Left **Pharmacy** Centre **Ambulance** Right **Policemen**

🔟 Security and Health

1 Emergencies
Call 113 for general emergencies; see the numbers listed in the box below for specific assistance. Most emergency services will be able to communicate with you in English if necessary.

2 Theft
Italy is relatively safe in terms of crime but tourism always attracts petty thefts. Keep an eye on your bags, especially in markets, on public transport and around tourist hot spots. Be wary of people begging with cardboard signs or newspapers: they are often used to distract you whilst your pockets are being emptied.

3 Drinking Water
Tap water in the towns and villages around the lakes is safe to drink but the taste is not always palatable. Out of habit, restaurants will always serve bottled water. Water labelled "acqua non potabile" is not drinkable.

4 Hospitals
Italian hospitals *(ospedale)* are efficient and the emergency departments *(pronto soccorso)* run on a triage system so the most serious cases are seen first. There may be a nominal charge (around €30) if your condition is not considered urgent but a visit to A&E is still the best way of getting treatment. Take your passport and, if you are a EU Citizen, EHI card along.

5 Pharmacies
Italian pharmacists *(farmacie)* are qualified to give medical advice and medication for minor health problems and are often the best first port of call. They stay open on a rota system and a list of the pharmacies on weekend or night-time duty is displayed by the door.

6 Dentists
A visit to the dentist in Italy is best avoided: treatment is not covered by the health service and prices are extortionate. English-speaking practices are available in the main towns but you would be better waiting until you get home. In an emergency, head for the local hospital.

7 Women Travellers
Italian men do look at and comment on women more than men in other countries but the flipside is that they are also often more courteous. Women may feel annoyed by the unwanted attention but should not usually feel threatened.

8 The Police
There are various police bodies in Italy but the three that visitors deal with are the Polizia Stradale on motorways, the Vigili Urbani who check parking and direct traffic, and the Caribinieri for general law and order. Thefts are reported to the latter, at a police station.

9 Sun Protection and Mosquitoes
The cool breezes blowing off the lakes can disguise the strength of the sun. Always apply high-factor sunscreens especially if you are going out on the water. Mosquitoes are a common problem in the summer in Milan and the southern reaches of the lakes; keep repellents and sprays to hand.

10 Lost Property
In villages it is worth checking at the police office in case any lost property *(oggetti smarriti)* has been handed in; you are unlikely to be so lucky in a larger town. For belongings left on boats or trains, your best bet is to check at the station or ticket office.

Emergency Numbers

Italy
- Carabinieri 112
- Ambulance 118
- Roadside assistance (not free) 116
- Fire services 115

Switzerland
- Police 117
- Fire, ambulance and accidents 118
- Roadside assistance 140

Left **Cappuccino** Centre **Cars by the lakeside** Right **Cheese**

TOP 10 Things to Avoid

1 Monday Sightseeing
Don't leave your sightseeing to a Monday. Most state museums and galleries, as well as the majority of private ones, throughout Italy are closed all day Monday. Some of the privately run lake villas and gardens are the exception to this rule but check carefully beforehand.

2 Driving in the Lakes Region
Driving around the lakes is best avoided as most towns and villages are car-free areas. There is insufficient parking and the lakeside roads are solid with slowly moving lines of cars and lorries. Public transport is good value, reliable and leaves you free to enjoy the views.

3 August
If possible, try not to book a trip to the Lakes for August. The two weeks around the public holiday on the 15th are the busiest. Prices rise significantly for accommodation and many hotels insist on a three-day minimum stay. Crowded sights and queues lead to a stressful holiday experience.

4 No Reservation
If you are planning to see Da Vinci's *The Last Supper* in Milan, make sure you book as far in advance as possible:

several months may be necessary for summer weekends. Likewise, accommodation on the lakes in August and during the design and fashion weeks in Milan needs to be reserved well ahead of time.

5 Cappuccino After Midday
A milky cappuccino – or *cappuccio* – is a breakfast drink in Italy. Italians are sticklers for convention and ordering a cappuccino later than midday will simply mark you down as an ignorant foreigner. If you want your coffee with milk, *café macchiato* is a good alternative.

6 Being Shy About Speaking Italian
You have got nothing to lose and most Italians will be more than pleased if you try. Just a few well-chosen words from the phrase book on *pp126–7* can help you to express yourself. Of course, understanding the reply is another matter altogether.

7 Winter
Most restaurants, hotels and sights around the lakes region are closed from November to Easter and ferry services are reduced to a minimum. However, there are many lively ski resorts further up the valleys and the Christmas markets in Bergamo,

Verona and Milan can be magical on crisp, frosty days.

8 Inappropriate Clothing
Places of worship throughout Italy insist on shoulders being covered (no vest t-shirts) and skirts or shorts reaching below the knee for both men and women. These rules are stringently adhered to with security personnel at the entrance to some churches turning away visitors who are inappropriately dressed.

9 Cheese and Fish
On the whole, cheese and fish are not eaten together in Italy. This means that parmesan or *grana padano* is rarely served with a seafood pasta or a fish risotto. Of course, there is no harm asking for cheese alongwith fish, but some waiters may raise an eyebrow.

10 Touristy Restaurants
Like tourist hot spots the world over, there are many restaurants around the lakes region that serve over-priced, poor quality food relying on the fact that you won't be returning anyway. The smarter way to find delicious food is to get away from the crowds, tail some locals or follow your nose. Part of the joy is discovering a great place by yourself.

Left **Public transport** Centre **Church of Sant'Ambrogio** Right **Takeaway food shop**

🔟 Budget Tips

1 Drink Standing Up
A drink at the bar is decidedly cheaper than one served at a table, especially an outside table where the surcharge is significant. Whether you want to down a quick expresso or while away time nibbling on the complimentary treats with an *aperitivo*, elbow yourself a little space at the bar.

2 Self-Cater
Picking up your basket and shopping for supplies can make you feel like a real local as well as save you cash. Street markets provide a wonderful array of fresh ingredients and even large supermarkets make an exciting alternative to those at home.

3 Public Transport
Forget hiring a car and paying for expensive petrol, parking and insurance, when there is good-value Italian public transport as a far better option. There are further discounts for over 60s, under 12s, sometimes for students and under 4s go free. Airport transfers, funicular railways and cable-car rides compliment the trinity of trains, buses and ferries.

4 Simple Restaurants
Italian food is simple, best when made with good, fresh ingredients. Local trattorias or small family-run restaurants can offer the best of this kind of cooking. Opt for the day's specials and wash it down with a carafe of excellent house wine. As well as saving money, the experience is likely to be more memorable.

5 Pay in Cash
To avoid paying extra fees for foreign transactions or exorbitant credit card rates, pay with cash. You will feel like a local too, as most Italians rarely use cards. Some hotels even offer a small discount for cash as they won't have to pay the card company's fees.

6 Avoid High Season
Peak season means exorbitant prices. May and September are delightful times to visit: the weather is warm, visitor numbers comparatively low and accommodation prices are significantly cheaper. Getting to the region should also be more economical than in the height of summer.

7 Put Together a Picnic
Takeaway food is found everywhere in Italy. A slice of pizza or fresh *focaccia* from the baker's or a *panino* made up from a *gastronomia* give you a delicious ready-made picnic in minutes. Alternatively, put together your own picnic basket from a local street market and round it all off with an ice cream.

8 Make the Most of Discounts
If you are over 60, under 26, a student, or a teacher and have ID to prove it, ask for a discount. Some places are strict about the ID they accept; others will happily waver large chunks of the cost of a ticket. Members of the National Trust and the Royal Horticultural Society should take their cards to the lakeside villas for discounts.

9 Free Attractions
Enjoy the picturesque beauty of the Italian lakes for free. Whatever your ability – mountain climbing, hill walking or a stroll along the promenade – there are routes for all levels throughout the region. And if you tire of the views – or the weather turns – churches and chapels can be fascinating and are free.

10 Get Away from the Crowds
Prices are always lower off the beaten track. Enjoy the tourist centres and then head away when it is time to eat. Lakeside restaurants and cafés charge top prices but you can enjoy the same views sitting on a bench having eaten elsewhere for much less.

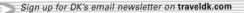

Left **Antipasto** Centre **Red wine** Right **Colourful *Gelateria* sign**

Dining Tips

1 Antipasto
Antipasto literally means "before the meal"; it is the appetizer course and it is also one of the best ways to try local specialities. A typical offering would be a plate of *affettati misti* (local salami and cured meats like bresaola and prosciutto) or a dish of marinated lake fish.

2 Primo
The choice of first courses (*primi*) will include rice and pasta dishes as well as soups. The pasta is often homemade and served with a sauce or stuffed like ravioli or tortellini and served with melted sage butter. Arborio rice, grown along the Po valley to the south of Milan, is combined with seasonal vegetables, fish or meat to make creamy risottos.

3 Secondo
The *secondo* or main course usually features a fish or meat dish and perhaps a little garnish. Meats include *manzo* (beef), *agnello* (spring lamb), *vitello* (veal), *pollo* (chicken), *cinghiale* (boar), *coniglio* (rabbit) and *anatra* (duck). For vegetables or a salad, you will need to ask for a side order (*contorno*) or *insalata* as well.

4 Coffee
Ordering a coffee in ritual-ridden Italy is a minefield. Frothy, white cappuccino is served for breakfast, a strong black shot of coffee (espresso) at any time of day. An Americano is similar to a filter coffee and caffè latte is very milky.

5 Cover Charges and Tipping
A cover charge is a ubiquitous addition to the bill here. It varies between one and five euros per person and often includes bread – regardless of whether you asked for it, want it or even eat it. For tipping, if there is no service charge included (*servizio incluso*) in the bill, it is customary to leave around a 10 per cent tip for a meal. For a coffee or drink, a few coins will suffice.

6 Wine and Water
As well as the wine list (*carta dei vini*), be aware that most places will have a decent house wine (*vino della casa*) that they will serve in full, half (*mezzo*) or quarter (*quarto*) carafes of either red (*rosso*) or white (*bianco*). Italians invariably drink and serve bottled water. Still water (*acqua naturale*) and sparkling (*acqua frizzante*) will be offered with any meal.

7 Slow Food
The Slow Food Movement (www.slowfood.it) was founded in 1986 by Carlo Petrini to promote and "rediscover the flavours and savors of regional cooking and banish the degrading effects of Fast Food." Look out for Slow-Food endorsed restaurant which will invariably serve well-cooked seasonal, local produce.

8 Gelaterie and Dolce
Of course desserts can vary hugely depending on the type of restaurant, but tiramisu is frequently on menus as is *torta* or *crostata di mela* (apple cake or tart). Once you have tried ice cream (*gelato*) that has been made on the premises (*produzione propria*) it is difficult to ever go back to the mass-produced alternatives. Follow the locals to find the best ice-cream shop in town.

9 Restaurant Types
Taverna, trattoria, *osteria* and locanda are all names for family-run, moderately priced establishments, but these days you'll have to look at the menu to determine the price and style of cooking. *Ristoranti* are, however, nearly always formal, pricey places.

10 Bars
Most Italian bars serve pastries and sandwiches alongside a morning cappuccino, espresso throughout the day and apéritifs in the evening.

Streetsmart

Left **Camping site near Monte Brione** Right **Youth hostel, Menaggio**

TOP 10 Accommodation Tips

Bed and Breakfast
Renting a room is an increasingly popular form of holiday accommodation in Italy. Prices and standards vary but the website www.bbitalia.it is a good first port of call, as are the *agriturismi* (farm stays) organizations or tourist offices.

Renting an Apartment or Villa
Share costs with friends and family and rent an apartment or villa. Not only will you have your own space, you can play at being Italian and self-cater from local markets. ⓢ *Cottages to Castles: 01622 775 217 • www.cottagestocastles. com • Interhome: +41 (0) 43 810 91 26 • www. interhome.co.uk • Italian Breaks: 020 8666 0407 • www.italianbreaks.com • Owners' Syndicate: 020 7401 1086 • www. ownerssyndicate.co.uk*

Hotels
This region of Italy offers everything from the most exclusive hotels in the world to plain establishments with shared facilities – and, of course, everything in between. The Italian terms *albergo, locanda* and *pensione* are pretty much inter-changeable translations of "hotel".

Agriturismi Stays
Staying on an *agriturismo* means staying on a working farm – in this region often a rice-growing or wine-making estate. They are usually inexpensive lodgings although some can be very luxurious. Accommodation can vary from a room with a shared bathroom to self-contained apartments. Activities are often on offer, from horse riding or cycling to wine-tasting and guided walks. ⓢ *Turismo Verde: 06 324 0111 • www.turismoverde. it; www.agriturist.com*

Room with a View
If you have your heart set on a lake view or any other specific request, make sure that you request it at the time of booking. Rooms often come with a small supplement, as do extra beds or cots.

Booking Ahead
In peak season (summer and Aug) many of the region's hotels get booked up. If you prefer to know exactly where you are going, make reservations in advance. Many tourist offices will help you book a last-minute room if you want to try your luck, although it may be a different price bracket than you were expecting.

Camping
This very popular camping destination offers something for everyone. Lakeside sites are invariably mini resorts with pools, places to eat, maybe even organized activities, but away from the water things can get simpler. Many places offer cabins and apartments as well as tents or tent pitches.

Monastery Stays
Staying in a working convent or monastery offers a well-priced option. Open to everyone regardless of gender or religion, decor is usually plain, beds are singles and all rooms have private bathrooms. Some establishments have curfews, however. ⓢ *www.monasterystays.com*

Hostels
Most major towns have the provision of shared dorms in cheap hostels. However, the Hostelling Association has hostels around the lakes that offer a sociable alternative to cheap hotels, with decent facilities at good prices. The HI Hostels at Menaggio, Bergamo, Riva, and Lugano are particularly worth checking out. ⓢ *www.hihostels.com*

Hidden Extras
By law, room prices for all seasons must be displayed in the hotel room (usually on the back of the door); taxes must also be stated. Check whether breakfast is included in the price you are quoted.

Left **Villa d'Este** Centre **Villa Feltrinelli** Right **Grand Hotel des Illes Borromees**

🔟 Luxury Hotels

1 Villa Sostaga
Set on a hillside above Lake Garda, the Villa Sostaga has a stunning panorama. The rooms are furnished with period pieces and there are extensive grounds, with a swimming pool. The well-priced restaurant serves quality meals on the terrace in summer. ⊗ *Via Sostaga 19, Gargnano, Lake Garda • Map R3 • 0365 791 218 • www. villasostaga.com • €€€€*

2 Villa Feltrinelli
One of the world's best hotels, this Liberty villa has a pool and grounds leading to Lake Garda. Its 13 rooms and handful of suites are furnished with antiques. ⊗ *Via Rimembranza 38–40, Gargnano, Lake Garda • Map R3 • 0365 798 000 • www.villafeltrinelli.com • €€€€€*

3 Villa Principe Leopoldo
In an elegant residential district just outside Lugano, this lakefront hotel boasts bright rooms and suites with lake views or gardens. The exclusive spa is the latest word in indulgent luxury. ⊗ *Via Montalbano 5, Lugano, Switzerland • Map L2 • +41 (0)91 985 88 55 • www. leopoldohotel.com • €€€€€*

4 Grand Hotel Villa Serbelloni
In an unbeatable location on Lake Como, this mid-19th-century hotel now boasts a Michelin-starred restaurant and two pools. ⊗ *Via Roma 1, Bellagio, Lake Como • Map N3 • 031 950 216 • www. villaserbelloni.com • €€€€€*

5 Villa Cortine
This Neo-Classical villa stands in formal lakeside parkland featuring Roman ruins, a tennis court and a pool. The comfortable rooms have parquet flooring and traditional furnishings. ⊗ *Via Grotte 6, Sirmione, Lake Garda • Map R5 • 030 990 5890 • www.palacehotelvillacortine.it • €€€€€*

6 Grand Hotel Fasano e Villa Principe
An opulent villa hotel dating from Gardone's hey day. The extensive park holds exotic palms and a pool with lake views. The spacious public rooms are formal but not stuffy and the bedrooms are classically decorated. ⊗ *Corso Zanardelli 190, Gardone Riviera • Map Q4 • 0365 290 220 • www.ghf.it • €€€€*

7 Villa d'Este
This has been a pleasure palace for much of its 500-year history. These days, wealthy guests and Hollywood celebrities come to enjoy the 25 acres of gardens and the lakeside luxury. ⊗ *Via Regina 40, Cernobbio, Lake Como • Map M4 • 031 3481 • www. villadeste.it • €€€€€*

8 Grand Hotel des Illes Borromees
One of the very first of the lake's Grand Hotels, this opulent Liberty confection has hosted international aristocracy and royalty since it opened in 1861. Bedrooms are decorated in sumptuous Napoleon-era decor. The hotel also boasts vast public spaces, lawns and swimming pools. ⊗ *Corso Umberto 1, 67 Stresa, Lake Maggiore • Map J3 • 0323 938 938 • www.borromees.it • €€€€€*

9 Villa dal Pozzo d'Annone
Given as a wedding gift in 1827, this exclusive retreat remains in the same family who lovingly nurture its historical treasures whilst maintaining a contemporary hotel with a relaxed, atmosphere. ⊗ *Strada del Sempione 5, Lake Maggiore • Map J4 • 0322 7255 • www.villadalpozzo dannone.com • €€€€€*

10 Locanda San Vigilio
Punta San Vigilio is one of the most bewitching corners in the lakes region. This homely inn has seen better days: the decor of the rooms is dated but the atmosphere is friendly and the location between the lake and olive groves truly breathtaking. ⊗ *Punta San Vigilio Garda, Lake Garda • Map R4 • 045 725 6688 • www. locanda-sanvigilio.it • €€€€€*

Price Categories

For a standard double room per night during tourist season, including taxes and service charges.

€	Under €100
€€	€100–€150
€€€	€150–€200
€€€€	€200–€250
€€€€€	over €250

Above **Leon d'Oro**

TOP 10 Lakeside Hotels

1 Il Sole
Drapes and heavy prints decorate the 14 well-appointed rooms in this family-run establishment on the banks of Lake Maggiore. An excellent restaurant, a large swimming pool and the nearby public ferry landing stage make this an ideal base for visitors to explore the region. Ⓢ *Piazza Venezia 5, Ranco, Lake Maggiore • Map J4 • 0331 976 507 • www. ilsolediranco.it • €€€€*

2 Gardesana
This three-star hotel has a dreamy location at the side of the tiny harbour in Torri del Benaco on Lake Garda. The decent, well-priced rooms have balconies and lovely lake views; service is friendly. Ⓢ *Piazza Calderini 20, Torri del Benaco, Lake Garda • Map R4 • 045 722 5411 • www. hotel-gardesana.com • €€€*

3 Hotel Verbano
Set in a wonderfully unique location on the Borromeo island of Isola dei Pescatori, the 12 bright, individually decorated rooms in this traditional *albergo* have polished wooden floors and soothing pastel decor. Wander around the peaceful island at will once the tourists have left in the evening. Ⓢ *Via Ugo Ara 2, Isola dei Pescatori, Lake Maggiore • Map J3 • 0323 30 408 • www.hotelverbano.it • €€€*

4 San Rocco
This hotel's highlight is its location – in a quiet part of the pretty village, right on the lake. The best of the contemporary rooms have lake views. Ⓢ *Via Gippini 11, Orta San Giulio, Lake Orta • Map J4 • 0322 911 977 • www. hotelsanrocco.it • €€€€*

5 Hotel Gardenia al Lago
A pretty family-run hotel in Gargnano on Lake Garda. Life here has a relaxed feel, with guests enjoying the waterfront patch of garden. Rooms are small but pleasantly furnished and some have balconies over the water. Ⓢ *Via Colletta 53, Gargnano, Lake Garda • Map R3 • 0365 71 195 • www. hotel-gardenia.it • €€*

6 Bellerive
This four-star hotel is along the waterfront, a short walk from the centre of Salò. Most rooms have balconies with lake views. There is an excellent restaurant called "100km" that sources all its ingredients from within 100 km (62 miles). Ⓢ *Via Pietro da Salò 11, Salò, Lake Garda • Map Q4 • 0365 520 410 • www. hotelbellerive.it • €€€*

7 Hotel Cannero
On the edge of the water, opposite the ferry-boat jetty, Hotel Cannero offers very comfortable rooms with wooden floors and coloured drapes. It also boasts a tennis court, a shady pool and a good lakeside restaurant. Ⓢ *Cannero, Lake Maggiore • Map K2 • 0323 788 046 • www. hotelcannero.com • €€*

8 Hotel Du Lac
Built in 1823, this attractive villa is tucked away in a corner of possibly the nicest village on Lake Como. It has bright public areas, tastefully decorated rooms and a vine-covered terrace. Ⓢ *Via del Prestino 4, Varenna, Lake Como • Map N2 • 0341 830 238 • www. albergodulac.com • €€€*

9 Il Vapore
Bright en suite rooms are decently furnished in this simple waterfront hotel in the backwater village of Torno on Lake Como. Well away from the crowds, Il Vapore also has a modest restaurant under the shade of plane trees. Ⓢ *Torno, Lake Como • Map M4 • 031 419 311 • www.hotelvapore.it • €€*

10 Leon d'Oro
The Leon d'Oro is worth a stay for its position alone: right over the water on the central square in bewitching Orta San Giulio. Many of the en-suite rooms offer glimpses of the lake. There is a restaurant downstairs. Ⓢ *Piazza Motta 42, Orta San Giulio, Lake Orta • Map J4 • 0322 911 991 • www. orta.net/leondoro • €€€*

Left **Hotel Catullo** Centre **Antica Locanda dei Mercanti** Right **Grifone**

🔟 Town- and Village-Centre Hotels

1 Hotel Catullo
A dusky pink three-star hotel in the village of Sirmione at the southern end of Lake Garda, with outside terraces, a private jetty and an attractive garden. All of the pleasant 56 bedrooms have balconies; decor is heavily patterned and traditional. ⊗ *Piazza Flaminia 7, Sirmione, Lake Garda • Map R5 • 030 9905811 • www.hotelcatullo.it • €€*

2 Hotel Torcolo
This 19-room hotel in Verona's centre is just steps away from the Arena. Pleasant, simple rooms are all double glazed and the car park is available for residents' use (20 euro per night). ⊗ *Vicolo Listone 3, Verona • Map H4 • 045 8007512 • www.hoteltorcolo.it • €€*

3 Antica Locanda dei Mercanti
This wonderful little bolt-hole is at the very centre of Milan, just minutes from the Duomo. There are no public areas but the bright rooms are individually furnished and breakfast is served in your room. ⊗ *Via San Tomaso 8, Milan • Map V3 • 02 805 4080 • www.locanda.it • €€€*

4 Grifone
This very simple, friendly two-star hotel is unbeatable for its price and its location right on the lake in Sirmione village. The attached fish restaurant has a lovely terrace. ⊗ *Via Bocchio 4, Sirmione, Lake Garda • Map R5 • 030 916 014 • €*

5 Mercure Palazzo Dolci
Well located in the lower town, this stylish modern chain hotel offers one of the best accommodation options in Bergamo. The staff is friendly and knowledgeable and the air-conditioned rooms are very comfortable. The hotel serves up delicious breakfast-buffets. ⊗ *Viale Papa Giovanni XXIII 100, Bergamo • Map D3 • 035 227 411 • www.mercure.com • €€*

6 Bulgari
Milan's best hotel offers all the style you could hope for from the design capital, combined with friendly discreet service. The hotel boasts an exclusive spa and it has a beautiful walled garden – the perfect place to wind down with an aperitivo on hot summer evenings. ⊗ *Via Privata Fratelli Gabba 7/b, Milan • Map W2 • 02 805 8051 • www.bulgarihotels.com • €€€€€*

7 Pironi
This charming hotel located in a restored Franciscan monastery is tucked away in the pretty winding lanes of Cannobio on Lake Maggiore. The 12 rooms are individually decorated and the cellars have been converted into an attractive wine bar. ⊗ *Via Marconi 35, Cannobio • Map K2 • 0323 70 624 • www.pironihotel.it • €€*

8 Del Duca
A small friendly hotel set in the heart of Como on a pretty cobbled square not far from the waterfront. All the pleasant rooms have wooden floors and spacious bathrooms; the best ones overlook the square. ⊗ *Piazza Mazzini 12, Como • Map M4 • 031 264 859 • www.albergodelduca.it • €€*

9 Casa Poli
This lovely boutique hotel in Mantova is located on cobbled lanes between the Palazzo Ducale and the Palazzo Te. The bedrooms are spacious with small en-suite shower rooms and there is an attractive outdoor courtyard garden with tables. ⊗ *Corso Garibaldi 32, Mantova • Map H6 • 0376.288.170 • www.hotelcasapoli.it • €€*

10 Dellearti Design Hotel
If you like your hotels all flat screens and contemporary colours, this swish place a couple of steps from the medieval splendour of central Cremona is the answer. The stylish rooms are individually designed and there is a gym, jacuzzi and a courtyard garden. ⊗ *Via Bonomelli 8, Cremona • Map E6 • 0372 23 131 • www.dellearti.com • €€*

Price Categories

For a standard double room per night during tourist season, including taxes and service charges.

	Under €100
€€	€100-€150
€€€	€150-€200
€€€€	€200-€250
€€€€€	over €250

Left **Friendly Rentals** Right **Residenza Patrizia**

TOP10 Guesthouses and Self-Catering

1 Bergamo Bed and Breakfast

A website that lists bed and breakfast options in Bergamo city and the hills and surrounding countryside including Lake Iseo: www.bedandbreakfastbergamo.com. Properties range from 19th-century palaces to suburban houses, from lakeside residences to medieval farmhouses.

2 Friendly Rentals

A well-organized Milan-based agency specializing in good quality self-catering flats in the city. There is a wide choice from studios to two-bed apartments. Prices are competitive and service friendly. Reservations can be from one night to six months. ◈ www.friendlyrentals.com

3 Silvio

A few minutes' walk away from Bellagio are a number of bright and simple rooms with bewitching views across Lake Como and above the excellent fish restaurant of the same name. Self-catering villas and apartments are also available in Bellagio itself. ◈ Via Carcano 12, Loppia, Lake Como • 031 951 018 • www.bellagiosilvio.com • €

4 Cottages to Castles

A small selection of villas are offered by this UK-based agency that has specialized in top-end

self-catering holidays for over 15 years. ◈ www.cottagestocastles.com

5 La Luna nel Porto

A lakefront house offering hotel rooms and good-sized self-catering apartments sleeping from one to four people. There are very pleasant waterside gardens and all the apartments have balconies with lake views or private terraces.
◈ Corso Italia 60, Stresa, Lake Maggiore
• Map J3 • 02 7600 8700 • www.lalunanelporto.it • €€

6 La Dolce Vita

A small villa in southern Milan near the trendy self-styled neighbourhood of Tortona zone. There are three twin or double rooms plus a pretty garden. ◈ Via Cola di Rienzo 3, Milan • Map N6 • 02 4895 2808 • www.ladolcevite.net • €€

7 Residenza Patrizia

These bright, well equipped apartments are attractively furnished and most have their own balcony or terrace. Guests can use the pool, spa and restaurant facilities of the hotel in the same appealing complex.
◈ Via Veneto Cannobio, Lake Maggiore • Map K2 • 0323 739 713 • www.residenzapatrizia.com • €€

8 B&B La Canarina

A charming B&B in the centre of Como just behind the lake. The bright

rooms are tastefully furnished and decorated in neutral colours and wrought-iron finishings with wooden floors. The bathrooms are attractive and modern. ◈ Via Manzoni 22, Como • Map M4 • 031 301 913 • www.bed-and-breakfast-como.it • €

9 Villa San Pietro

An Italian-French couple runs this relaxing B&B in the small town of Montichiari, near Brescia. Traditional solid wood antiques decorate the 17th-century building and rooms are spacious. Breakfast (and dinner on request) is served in the frescoed dining room or outside in the courtyard. ◈ Via San Pietro 25, Montichiari, Brescia • Map F5 • 030 961232 • www.abedandbreakfastinitaly.com• €

10 Dimora Bolsone

This 15th-century renovated manor house set in the lush hillside of Lake Garda has bright spacious rooms with stunning views over Lake Garda. Extensive gardens complete with waterfalls and shaded paths surround the ancient stone house offering a wonderfully restful break. Bicycles are available for hire.
◈ Via Panoramica 23, Gardone Riviera, Lake Garda • Map Q4 • 0365 210 22 • No children under 12 • www.gardalake.it/dimorabolsone/ • €

Price Categories

For a standard, double room per night (with breakfast if included), taxes and extra charges.

€	under €100
€€	€100–€150
€€€	€150–€200
€€€€	€200–€250
€€€€€	over €250

Above **View from Cascina Borgo Francone, Pian di Spagna**

Agriturismi

1 Borgo San Donino
This wine-making estate near Lake Garda offers a few rooms and several self-catering apartments with their own outside spaces. The apartments have bright, wooden interiors and serene surroundings. Facilities include a swimming pool, restaurant and wine tastings.
Ⓢ *Agriturismo Borgo San Donino, Cascina Capuzza, Desenzano del Garda • Map Q5 • 030 991 0279 • www. selvacapuzza.it • €*

2 I Marroni
Located just 10 km (6 miles) from the eastern shore of Lake Maggiore, this low-key farm cultivates raspberries and blueberries in summer and chestnuts in autumn. There are two comfortable apartments set in acres of land. Good for walks and treks.Ⓢ *Loc. Gaggiolo, Orino, Varese • Map L4 • 0331 631 355 • www. imarroni.it • €*

3 Pratello
Surrounded by vines and with views over Lake Garda, the extensive grounds at this relaxing *agriturismo* in the Moreniche hills include a swimming pool, cantina and seasonal restaurant. Rooms sleeping from 2 to 6 people are available. Ⓢ *Via Pratello 26, Padenghe sul Garda • Map Q5 • 030 990 7005 • www.pratello.com • €€*

4 Hobby Farm Ardizzone
This 15th-century fortified farmhouse on a hillside has stables and an ostrich farm. It offers various self-catering apartments in the ancient stone buildings as well as local cooking on request. Ⓢ *Cascina Grumello, Frazione Nese, Alzano Lombardo, Bergamo • Map E3 • 035 510 060 • www.hobbyfarms.it • €€*

5 Locanda del Glicine Antico
A splendid 18th-century manor house with three double rooms. The majestic wisteria the house is named for clambers through the courtyard. Lake Maggiore is nearby and there are pleasant walks through the surrounding woods. Ⓢ *Via Mazzini 10, Castello Cabiaglio, Varese • Map L4 • 339 152 3797 • www.locanda-delglicineantico.it • €*

6 Cascina Borgo Francone
These apartments are located in the natural reserve of Pian di Spagna, making it an ideal location for bird watching, horse riding and cycling. There is a heated indoor swimming pool and acres of woods to explore.
Ⓢ *Cascina Borgo Francone, Pian di Spagna, Gera Lario, Lake Como • Map P1 • 334 6431 783 • www.cascina-borgofrancone.com • €€€*

7 Il Bagnolo
Nine pretty rooms are available in this stylish *argriturismo* on a quiet hillside above Lake Garda. The exclusive restaurant here serves locally sourced food and wine.
Ⓢ *Bagnolo di Serniga, Salò, Lake Garda • Map Q4 • 0365 20 290 • www.ilbagnolo.it • €*

8 Eremo Relais
Located above Bardolino with splendid views over Lake Garda, the Eremo Relais is set among olive trees within a vineyard. This relaxed home offers three double rooms, far removed from the busy lake. Ⓢ *Strada della Rocca 2, Bardolino, Lake Garda • Map R5 • 045 721 1391 • www. eremorelais.com • €*

9 Agrituristico Mantovano
Among the lakes and rivers around Mantova are some of the region's best *agriturismi*. This group of farm tourism operators are well organized and offer more than 50 options. Ⓢ *Largo Porta Pradella 1, Mantova • Map H6 • 0376 324 889 • www.agriturismomantova.it*

10 Le Frise
This working farm to the north of Lake Iseo offers rooms in pretty stone buildings along with a cosy restaurant. Ⓢ *Rive dei Balti, Artogne, Val Camonica • Map F3 • 0364 598 298 • www.lefrise.it • €*

Agriturismi *are working farms that also provide accommodation for holidaymakers.*

Price Categories	
For a standard camping unit for two people and a pitch.	€ under €20
	€€ €20–€30
	€€€ €30–€40
	€€€€ €40–€50
	€€€€€ over €50

Above **Camping Nanzel at Limone sul Garda**

🔟 Campsites

1 Camping Isolino
A well organized complex on the shores of Lake Maggiore offering bungalows, tents and caravan pitches. Amenities include two pools, water slides, sports and organized activities, a private lake beach as well as refreshment options. ✹ *Via Per Feriolo, 25–28924 Verbania, Lake Maggiore • Map Q4 • 0323 496 080 • www. campingisolino.it • €€€€*

2 Camping Bella Italia
Within walking distance of Peschiera on Lake Garda, this spacious site has bungalows, caravans and tents with plenty of greenery. There is also a water park, a lakeside beach and sports and entertainment facilities. ✹ *Via Bella Italia 2, Peschiera del Garda • Map R5 • 045 640 0688 • www.camping-bellaitalia. eu • €€€*

3 Camping Valle Romantica
On the river bank, just outside Cannobio, this campsite has beautiful, mature grounds. Accommodation options include rustic apartments and new caravans while the café in the old farmhouse has tables outside under the wisteria. ✹ *Camping Valle Romantica, Cannobio Lake Maggiore • Map K2 • 0323 71 360 • www.riviera-valleromantica.com • €€€€*

4 Camping Nanzel
A simple site just outside Limone on the north-western shore of Lake Garda. Pitches are among olive groves and the site has its own beach. ✹ *Via 4 Novembre 3, Limone sul Garda • Map S2 • 0365 954 155 • www. campingnanzel.it • €€*

5 Camping Village Città di Milano
Bungalows and tent pitches make for a cheap camping base just outside Milan. There is also a children's playground, picnic area and a pizzeria. ✹ *Via Gaetano Airaghi 61, Milan • Map N6 • 02 4820 7017 • www. campingmilano.it • €€*

6 Camping Bellagio
This is a refreshingly underdeveloped site outside Bellagio on the hills overlooking Lake Como. Camping is in two green fields, facilities are simple and it is within walking distance of a village with shopping and dining facilities. ✹ *Map N3 • 031 951 325 • www.bellagio-camping.com • €€*

7 Camping Orta
Less than 2 km (1 mile) outside Orta, this little site offers bungalows and caravans as well as tent pitches. The terraced grassy pitches lead down to the road and lakeside beach. ✹ *Via Domodossola 28, Orta San Giulio • Map J4 • 0322 90 267 • www. campingorta.it • €€€*

8 Campeggio Villagio Gefara
Located at the northern end of Lake Como, this bustling campsite offers apartments, caravans and tents. The long stretch of lake beach is backed by a grassy area shaded by trees. ✹ *Via Case Sparse 230, Domaso, Lake Como • Map N1 • 0344 96163 • www.campinggcfara.it • €*

9 Camping Conca d'Oro
A pleasant campsite on the shores of Lake Maggiore with lovely views, 210 tent pitches and caravans for hire. The beach is particularly suitable for children as there are organized activities for under-16s. There is also a small supermarket, bar and restaurant. ✹ *Via Quarantadue Martiri 26, Feriolo, Baveno, Lake Maggiore • Map J3 • 0323 288116 • www.concadoro.it • €€€€*

10 Camping Delta
A quality site on the banks of Lake Lugano that has attractive grounds and good facilities. There are children's activities, watersports equipment for hire, swimming pools and tennis courts as well as a pizzeria and an attractively located bar. ✹ *Camping Delta – Via Respini 7, Locarno, Switzerland • Map L1 • (+41) 91 7516 081 • www. campingdelta.com • €€€€*

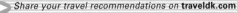

General Index

Page numbers in **bold** type refer to main entries

212 Bar Code, Bergamo 53

A
Abbazia di Piona 72
Accademia Carrara 76, 77
accommodation
 agriturismi 111, 116
 campsites 117
 guesthouses and
 self-catering 115
 lakeside hotels 113
 luxury hotels 112
 town- and village-centre
 hotels 114
Adige, river 20
A Farewell to Arms 11, 52
Agrituristico Mantovano 116
airports 103
Al Boeuc 67
Al Mascaron 53
Alpinia Botanic Garden 66
Alprose Chocolate Factory 54
Alto Ticino 65
Anema e Cozze 99
Angel 44
Angera 64, 66
Antica Locanda dei Mercanti 114
Antica Locanda Mincio 91
Antica Trattoria alle Rose 91
Antipasto 110
antiques fairs 97
apartment rentals 111
Aqua Paradise Park 47, 50, 89
architects
 Biffi, Andrea 8
 Crivelli, Giovanni Angelo 8
 Terragni, Giuseppe 15
Arco 88, 89
The Arena 21, 33, 90
Argegno 34, 41, 72, 74
Arlecchino 25
Arona 64
artists & sculptors
 artist visitors to Como 72
 Caravaggio 45, 93

artists & sculptors (cont.)
 d'Agrate, Marco 18
 da Pancale, Masolino 45
 da Vinci, Leonardo 17, 44, 93, 94, 95
 della Francesco, Piero 93
 Hayez, Francesco 71
 Luini, Bernardino 64
 Mantegna, Andrea 16, 93
 Michelangelo 17, 93
 Pisanello 20, 77
 Raphael 16
 Sanmicheli 20
 Wallinger, Mark 19, 44
 Zeffirelli, Franco 19, 44
 Zuccarelli, Francesco 8
Ascona 11, 65
Atrio di Diana 9, 66
Augustus, emperor 32

B
baby's needs 102
Il Bagnolo 116
Bagolino 27, 84, 86
Bagòss carnival 26, 27
Bagòss cheese 27
banks 106
Bar Bianco 98
Barchetta 75
Bardolino 29, 36, 88
Bar Radetzy 98
bars & cafés 52
Basilica di San Giulio 13, 36
Battistero Paleocristiano 18
Baveno 64
bed and breakfast 111
Bellagio 23, 70–75
Bellagio, Lake Como 47, 48, 59, 112
Bellano 74
Bellerive 91, 113
Bellinzona 55, 65
Bergamo 7, **24–25**, 76–81
Bergamo Bed and Breakfast 115
Bergamo, Brescia and Lake Iseo 76–81
 restaurants 81
Bergamo Funicular 57
Le Biciclette 98
boat trips
 Como 14, 15, 56
Bocchia, Ettore 75

Borgo San Donino 116
Borromeo, Cardinal Carlo 11
Borromeo, Cardinal Federico 94
Borromeo Chapel 8
Borromeo, Giovanni 8
Borromeo, Vitaliano 8
La Botte 43, 67
Bottega del Vino 91
boutiques 54
Brera and Moscova 97
Brescia 32, 33, 76–81
Brienno 74, 75
Brunate 14, 34, 71
Brunate to Torno, Lake Como 34
Buca del Gabbia 98
budget tips 109
Bulgari 114
Bureaux de Change 106
bus services 103

C
cablecar, Monte Baldo 50
Campeggio Villagio Gefara 117
camping 111
Camping Bellagio 117
Camping Bella Italia 117
Camping Conca d'Oro 117
Camping Delta 117
Camping Isolino 117
Camping Nanzel 117
Camping Orta 117
Camping Valle Romantica 117
Camping Village Città di Milano 117
canals of Milan 17
Cangrande II 20
Cannero 10, 11, 62, 63, 64
Cannero Riviera 10, 11
Cannobio 10, 11, 63, 64, 66
Cannobio beach 41
Cannobio, Lake Maggiore 34, 47, 115
canoeing, Lake Idro 27
Cantina della Vetra 95, 99
canyoning 39
Caravaggio 45, 93
Carlo II 8
Carnival 27, 36, 87
Casa di Giulietta 20, 88
Casa Mazzanti 90

Casa Poli 114
Cascina Borgo Francone 116
cash discounts 109
Casoncelli or Casonsei 42
Cassoeûla 42
Castello di Vezio, Varenna 23, 51
Castello Scaligero, Malcesine 90
Castello Scaligero, Torri del Benaco 90
Castello Sforzesco 17, 51, 93
Castelvecchio 20, 86
Catullus 28
Cavallino 91
Il Cavatappi 75
Centovalli, Lake Maggiore 34
Centovalli Railway 10, 62, 63, 65
Centro Lago and its villages 7, **22–23**
Centro Lago 7, 22, 56
Cernobbio 52, 74, 112
Certosa di Pavia 40, 92, 95
Charlemagne, King 32
Chiese, river 26, 27
children's attractions 50
Chocolat 98
Churchill, Winston 88
church and chapels see places of worship
Il Cigno 99
Città Alta 25, 79, 81
Città Bassa 24
clothing 102, 108
Clusone Jazz Festival 36
coaches to Italy 103
Cocktail Bar, Villa Cortine Palace Hotel, Sirmione 52
coffee 108, 110
La Colombetta 75
Colonne di San Lorenzo, Milan 33
Como 6, **14–15**
Como e Lugano boat trip 57
Como funicular 71
Constantine, emperor 32
Cooperativa Città Alta 43, 81
Corso Como 10 Café, Milan 52
Corso di Porta Ticinese 96
Cotoletta alla Milanese 43

Cova 98
cover charges and tipping 110
credit cards 106
crime 107
Crotto dei Platani 75
cruises, Lake Iseo 76, 79
La Cucina della Marianna 75
culinary specialities 42
currency 102, 106
cycling in the mountains 57, 103
cycling routes
along the canals - Milan to the Certosa di Pavia 40
around Malcesine, Lake Garda 40
around Menaggio, Lake Como 41
around Monte Isola, Lake Iseo 41
Gargnano to Limone via Tignale, Lake Garda 40
Mincio to Peschiera del Garda 40
Monte Mottarone, Lake Maggiore 41
through the Franciacorta Vineyards 41
through the Ossola Valley 40

D
d'Annunzio, Gabriele 90
da Vinci, Leonardo 17, 44, 93, 94, 95
The Dead Christ 44, 93
Dei Cigni 67
Del Duca 114
Dellearti Design Hotel 114
dentists 107
Desenzano 29, 88, 91
Design Café 98
desserts 110
dialling codes 104, 106
Dimora Bolsone 115
discounts 109
La Dolce Vita 115
Donizetti, Gaetano 25, 78
drinking tips 109
drinks 53
driving
driving in the Lakes region 103, 108
driving licence 102
rules of the road 103

driving to Italy 103
I Due Roccoli 81
Due Stelle 81
The Duomo, Como 14, 71
The Duomo, Cremona 96
The Duomo, Milan 16, **18–19**, 92, 93, 95
Battistero Paleocristiano 18
construction 19
façade 18
La Madonnina 19
Nail from the Cross 18
roof terraces 19
Scurolo di San Carlo 18
St Bartholomew Flayed 18
Sundial 19
Treasury 18
Via Dolorosa 19
The Duomo, Verona 20

E
electrical appliances 102
Emanuele I, Vittorio 33
emergency numbers 107
Eremo Relais 116
Eros and Psyche 71

F
factory outlets 55, 97
ferry services 62, 103
Festa del Lago 37
Festa dell'uva 36
Festa del Torrone 37
festivals 36
Film Festival, Locarno 36
films shot in the region
Casino Royale 72
Star Wars Episode II 72
Fontana di Madonna, Verona 33
Frederick I, emperor 32
free attractions 109
Friendly Rentals 115
Le Frise 116
funicular 14
funicular, Bergamo 25, 57, 76, 77

G
Gabbani Delicatessen 54
Galleria degli Arazzi 9
Galleria Vittorio Emanuele II 17, 54, 97
GAMEC 25, 44
Gandria 56, 65
Gardaland 50, 88

Garda 85
Gardens 48
Gardesana 91, 113
Gargnano 27, 40, 84, 86, 90, 112, 113
gelati 51, 110
Giardini Pubblici 51
Giardino d'Amore 9
Giardino Giusti 89
Gold Bar 52
golf 38
Golfo Borromeo 63
Gorgonzola 43, 55
Grana Padano 42
Grand Hotel des Illes Borromees 52, 112
Grand Hotel Fasano e Villa Principe 112
Grand Hotel Villa Serbelloni 75, 112
Gravedona 47, 74
Gravedona Beach and Lido 47
Greenway del Lago di Como 34
Grifone 28, 114
Grotte di Catullo 28, 33
Grottoes, Isola Bella 9

H
H-Club Diana Bar, Milan 52
Hayez, Francesco 71
Heller Garden 49, 89
Hemmingway, Ernest 11, 52
high season 104, 109
hiking 26, 27, 39
historical figures 32
Hobby Farm Ardizzone 116
horse riding 38
hospitals 107
hostels 111
Hotel Cannero 113
Hotel Catullo 114
Hotel Du Lac 113
Hotel Gardenia al Lago 113
hotels see accommodation
Hotel Torcolo 114
Hotel Verbano 67, 113

I
Idro 7, 26, 27, 88
insurance 102
Internet 106

Isola Bella 6, **8–9**, 48, 62
Isola Comacina 23, 35, 37, 72, 75
Isola di Garda 89
Isola Madre 49, 62, 66
Isola San Giulio 6, 12, 34, 66
Isole Borromeo 36, 60, 62, 63, 66
Isole di Brissago 11, 49, 63

J
Joia 99
Josephine 8
Just Cavalli Café 52

K
kayaking 38
kitesurfing 10

L
Lake Como 7, 14, 22, 23, 70–75
Lake Como and Around 70–75
    restaurants 75
    towns and villages 74
Lake Como ferries 23, 56
lake fish 42
Lake Garda 7, 26, 27, 84–90
Lake Garda and Around 84–91
    buildings 90
    parks and gardens 89
    restaurants 91
Lake Garda ferries 86
Lake Idro 7, 26, 27, 88
Lake Idro and the Valvestino 7, **26–27**
Lake Iseo 7, 76, 77, 78, 79
Lake Ledro 84, 85, 88
Lake Lugano 41, 57, 65
Lake Maggiore 6, 8, 10, 19, 52, 59, 60–67
Lake Maggiore and Around 60–67
    beauty spots 66
    restaurants 67
    Swiss side 65
    towns and villages 64
Lake Maggiore Express 10, 56, 60, 62, 63
Lake Mergozzo 64, 67
Lake Orta 6, 12, 38, 55, 60, 61, 67, 113

Lake Valvestino 26
language 105
La Luna nel Porto 115
The Last Supper 17, 44, 93, 95, 98, 102, 108
    Santa Maria delle Grazie monastery 17
Laveno 63, 64
Lawrence, D.H.
    Twilight in Italy 86
Lazise 29, 50
Lecco 36, 74
Leon d'Oro 13, 113
The Lido delle Bionde, Sirmione 28, 46
Lido Giardino 46
Limone sul Garda 84, 87, 117
The Liston, Verona 88
Locanda del Glicine Antico 116
Locanda dell'Isola Comacina 75
Locanda San Vigilio 46, 112
Locarno 11, 34, 36, 56, 62, 63, 65, 117
Locarno cable car and chair lift 56
Lombardy 7, 26, 92–99
lost property 107
Lugano 41, 54, 55, 56, 57, 65, 103, 111, 112, 117
Luini, Bernardino 10, 64, 98
Luino 11, 64
    Wednesday market 11

M
Madonna with Child, Angels, Saints and Federico da Montefeltro 93
Madonna and Francesco and Giulio 13
Madonna and Saints 21
La Madonnina 19
Malcesine 40, 50, 57, 84, 87, 90
Manerba 46
Mantegna, Andrea 16, 44
Manzoni, Alessandro 74
maps 104
Marco d'Agrate 18
I Marroni 116
Masolino da Pancale 45
Masuelli San Marco 99
Maximian, emperor 33

membership cards 102
Menaggio 23, 38, 41, 46, 74, 75
Mercato Wagner 97
Mercure Palazzo Dolci 114
Mergozzo 64, 67
Michelangelo 17, 93
  Rondanini Pietà 17
Milan 7, 11, **16–17**, 18, 19, 54, 55
Milan and Southern Lombardy 92–99
  cafés and bars 98
  churches 95
  restaurants 99
  shopping in Milan 97
Missoltini 43
Mistral 75
mobile phones 106
monastery stays 111
Monte Baldo 35, 38, 40, 50, 57, 87
Monte Baldo cable car 57
Monte Bisbino 74
Monte Brè 56
Monte Generoso 65
Monte Isola 35, 41, 76, 77, 78, 79
Monte Mottarone 40, 41, 60, 63, 66
Monte Rochetta 85
Monte San Prino 22, 23
mountain biking 38
Museo Bagatti Valsecchi 96
Museo Civico 15, 45, 87
Museo Donizettiano 25, 76, 78
Museo Poldi Pezzoli 96
Museo Stradivariano and Sala dei Violini 96
museums & galleries
  Accademia Carrara 76, 77
  Castello Sforzesco 17, 50, 51, 93
  Castelvecchio 20, 86
  Galleria degli Arazzi 9
  GAMEC 25, 44
  Museo Bagatti Valsecchi 96
  Museo Civico 15, 45, 87
  Museo della Città 78
  Museo Donizettiano 25, 78
  Museo Poldi Pezzoli 96

museums & galleries (cont.)
  Museo Stradivariano and Sala dei Violini 96
  Ogliari Transport Museum 64
  Pinacoteca Ambrosiana 92, 94
  Pinacoteca di Brera 16, 92, 93
  Triennale 92, 94
musicians
  Donizetti, Gaetano 25, 78
  Verdi 21, 72
Mussolini, Benito 33

N
Nail from the Cross 18
Napoleon 8, 16, 32, 73, 93
Navigli District 16, 17, 92, 94
Nesso 74
Northern Lake Maggiore 6, **10–11**

O
Ochina Bianca 43, 99
Ogliari Transport Museum 64
Olive Groves, Sirmione 89
Omegna 55
opening hours 104
opera tours 105
Orangery Café 73
Orrido di Sant'Anna, Cannobio 10, 11, 34, 41
Orrido di Sant'Anna, Lake Maggiore 34, 41
Orta, Wednesday market 12
Orta San Giulio 6, **12–13**, 60, 61, 64
Osteria Al Bianchi 43, 81
Osteria di Via Solata 81
Osteria il Gallo 91
outdoor sports 38
spectator sports tours 105
sports and races 39

P
Il Paiolo 81
Palazzo della Comunità 13
Palazzo della Ragione 25, 79
Palazzo Ducale 96, 114
Palazzo Maffei 90
Palazzo Pretorio 90

Palazzo Te, Mantova 92, 95
Palazzo Terragni 15
paragliding 38
Parco Baia delle Sirene 89
Parco Grotta Cascata Varone 89
Parco Nazionale delle Incisioni Rupestri 78
Parco Sempione 16, 52, 96, 98
passports 102
Pescallo 22, 71
Peschiera del Garda 28, 117
pharmacies 107
Piazza delle Erbe 21, 33, 90
Piazza Motta 13, 67
Piazza Vecchia 25, 77, 79
Piccolo Lago 67
picnics 109
La Piemontese 67
Piero della Francesco 93
Pietà 10, 11, 17, 93
Pinacoteca Ambrosiana 92, 94
Pinacoteca di Brera 16, 92, 93
Pironi 114
Pisanello 20, 77
pizza 51
places of worship
  Basilica di San Giulio 13, 36
  Borromeo Chapel 8
  church of San Giacomo, Bellagio 22
  church of San Giorgio, Bagolino 27
  church of San Giovanni 74
  churches of Milan 95
  The Duomo, Como 14
  The Duomo, Cremona 96
  The Duomo, Milan 16, 92, 93
  The Duomo, Verona 20
  Renaissance Portinari Chapel 95
  San Fermo 20, 21
  San Francesco 12, 90
  San Lorenzo alle Colonne 95, 96
  San Pietro in Mavino, Sirmione 28, 29
  Sant'Abbondio 15

places of worship (cont.)
Sant'Ambrogio 17, 36, 95, 96, 109
Sant'Anastasia 20
Sant'Eustorgio 95
Santa Maria del Tiglio 74
Santa Maria delle Grazie 17, 95
Santa Maria Maggiore and Cappella Colleoni 24
Santa Maria Maggiore, Bergamo 78
Santa Maria Maggiore, Sirmione 28
Po, river 17, 92, 94
Polenta 42
police 107
Ponte Caffero 26
Ponte Rosso 99
Porta dei Leoni 33
Portici del Comune 98
Portrait of a Musician 44, 45
postal services 106
Pratello 116
Primo 37, 110
public garden (Arco) 89
public holidays 37, 104
public transport 109
Punta San Vigilio 46, 53, 88, 89, 112

Q
Quadrilatero d'Oro 17, 54, 97

R
races 39
Ranco 10, 64, 67, 113
Raphael 16, 44
religious figures
Borromeo, Cardinal Carlo 11
Borromeo, San Carlo 18
Sant'Abbondio 15
St Ambrose 17, 18
St Augustine 18
St Bartholomew 18
St Fermo 21
St Francis of Assisi 12
St Julius (San Giulio) 13
St Rustico 21
Renaissance Portinari Chapel 95
renting an apartment or villa 111
reservations 102
Residenza Patrizia 115

restaurants
types 110
around Bergamo, Brescia and Lake Iseo 81
around Lake Como 75
around Lake Garda 91
around Lake Maggiore 67
for local dishes 43
Restel de Ferr 43, 91
rice cultivation 94
Rinascente 16, 97
Risotto alla Milanese 43
Ristorante 100km 43, 91
Ristorante Cracco 99
Il Ristorante di Paolo 43, 75
Riva del Garda 35, 84, 85, 87, 89, 90, 91, 105
The Rocca 24, 25, 29
Rocca Borromeo 9, 61
Rocca Scaligera 29, 85, 90
rock art, Capo di Ponte 44, 78
Roman sites, Brescia 78
Roman Temple, Brescia 33
Romeo and Juliet 21
rowing on Lake Orta 12
La Rucola 91

S
Sacro Monte di Ossuccio 70, 73
Sacro Monte di San Francesco 12
Sacro Monte, Orta San Giulio 34
Sagra di San Giovanni 36
sailing and windsurfing 38
Sala da Ballo 8, 9
Sala delle Medaglie 8, 9
Sala di Napoleone 8
Salò 81, 84, 86, 87, 91
San Babila 54
San Carlo Borromeo 18
San Fedele 14, 15, 96
San Fermo 20, 21
San Francesco 12, 90
San Lorenzo alle Colonne 95, 96
Sanmicheli 20
San Pancrazio 11, 49
San Pietro in Mavino 29
San Rocco 26, 91, 113

Sant'Abbondio 15
Santa Caterina del Sasso 36, 62, 66
Santa Lucia 37
Santa Maria degli Angeli 65
Santa Maria delle Grazie 16, 17, 95
Santa Maria del Tiglio 74
Santa Maria Maggiore and Cappella Colleoni 24
Santa Maria Maggiore, Bergamo 78
Santa Maria Maggiore, Sirmione 28
Sant'Ambrogio, Milan 17, 36, 95, 96
Sant'Anastasia 20
Sant'Apollinare 11
Sant'Eustorgio 95
Santuario della Pietà, Cannobio 11
San Vigilio 46, 53, 76, 77, 79, 81, 88, 89
San Zeno Maggiore 21, 53
La Scala 16, 36, 96
Scurolo di San Carlo 18
Secondo 110
senior citizens 105
Sentiero dei Contrabbandieri 27
Settimane Musicali di Stresa e del Lago Maggiore 36
Shakespeare, William 20
shopping 54–55
shopping in Bellagio 23
shopping in Bergamo 24
Sigurta Giardino, Valeggio sul Mincio, Verona 89
silk centre 15
Silvio 43, 75, 81, 115
Sirmione 7, 28, 29, 46, 52, 84, 85
Sirmione and Southern Lake Garda 7, **28–29**
skiing 39
Slow Food 99, 110
snowboarding 38
Il Sole 67, 113
La Sosta 99
Spazio Armani 97
special interest holidays 105
spectator sports and races 39

St Ambrose 17, 18
Stanza dello Zuccarelli 8
St Augustine 18
St Bartholomew 18
St Bartholomew Flayed
  18
steamer trip, Garda 50
St Fermo 21
St Francis in Meditation
  45
St Francis of Assisi 12
*St George Preparing to
  Save the Maiden* 20
St Julius (San Giulio) 13
La Streccia 43, 67
street markets 55, 97
Stresa 8, 9, 11, 36, 56, 60,
  62, 63, 67
Stresa Music Festival 9
Stresa's Promenade 66
St Rustico 21
study tours 105
Sunday market, Cannobio
  10
sun protection 107
Supper at Emmaus 93
swimming spots 46–47
Swissminiatur 50
Switzerland 65

T
Taleggio 42, 55
Taverna San Vigilio, Lake
  Garda 53
Teatro Massimo 8, 9, 60
Teatro Romano 21, 33
Teatro Sociale 25, 79, 80
telephones 106
Tempio Capitolino 44, 76,
  78
Terrace Bar, Villa d'Este,
  Lake Como 52
time 102
tipping 110
Torno 34, 74, 113
The Torrazzo, Cremona 92,
  94
Torre dei Lamberti 21
Torri del Benaco 46, 47,
  86, 88, 90, 91
Torri del Benaco Beach,
  Lake Garda 46
Toscolano, river 26
Tourist Boards 104
tourist information 104
train rides
  Centovalli Railway 10,
  34, 60, 62, 63, 65

train rides (cont.)
  Como funicular 71
  funicular 14
  funicular, Bergamo 25,
  57, 76, 77
  Lake Maggiore Express
  10, 62
  Il Trenino 13
  Treno Blu 57, 78
train services 103
trains to Italy 103
Trattoria Milanese 43, 99
Il Trenino 13
Treno Blu 57, 78

U
UNESCO World Heritage
  Sites
  Bellinzona 65
  Parco Nazionale delle
  Incisioni Rupestri 78
  Sacro Monte di
  Ossuccio 73

V
Val Camonica 38, 44, 76,
  78, 80, 116
Val Cannobio, Lake
  Maggiore 34
Valle Cannobina 66
Valle Maggia 65
Valvestino 7, 26, 88
Il Vapore 113
Varenna 23, 37, 70–75
Vasco da Gama 81
La Vecchia Arona 67
Vecchia Varenna 75
Verbania 49, 60, 61, 63,
  67
Verdi 21, 72
  Aïda 21
Verona 7, **20–21**, 29, 32,
  53, 84, 86, 88, 89, 90,
  91
Verona Card 20
Vesta 26
Via Dolorosa 19, 44
Via Garibaldi 100
Via Olina 12, 13
Villa Carlotta 22, 34, 48,
  70, 71, 73
Villa Carlotta, Tremezzo 22,
  70, 71
Villa Cipressi 48
Villa Cortine 52, 112
Villa Crespi 67
Villa dal Pozzo d'Annone
  112

Villa del Balbianello, Lenno
  23, 48, 72
Villa della Porta Bozzolo,
  Casalzuigno 66
Villa d'Este 38, 52, 74,
  112
Villa Feltrinelli 86, 112
Villa Fiordaliso 91
Villa Geno 15
Villa Melzi 48, 70, 73
Villa Monastero, Varenna
  71
Villa Olmo 14
Villa Principe Leopoldo
  112
Villa Romana, Desenzano
  29, 33
Villa San Pietro 115
Villa Serbelloni, Bellagio
  22, 49, 72, 112
Villa Sostaga 112
Villa Taranto 49, 60, 61
Vineria Cozzi 81
Visconti, Gian Galeazzo
  19
Il Vittoriale 89, 90

W
walks 105
walking trails 34
The Walls 25
water 107
weather 104
websites 104
windsurfing
  Pino 10
  Torbole 50, 51
wine 110
  wines of Southern
  Garda 29
wine outlets 54
wine-tasting 105
Winged Victory Statue,
  Brescia 33, 44, 78
women travellers 107
works of art 44
writers and poets
  Catullus 28
  Hemmingway, Ernest
  11, 52
  Lawrence, D.H. 86
  Manzoni, Alessandro 74

Z
Zeffirelli, Franco 19, 44
Zucca 98
Zuccarelli, Francesco 8

Acknowledgments

The Author
Lucy Ratcliffe is a travel writer and translator specializing in the northern Italian Lakes. For over 10 years she has travelled and lived in the region, writing numerous guidebooks as well as translating texts on contemporary architecture.

Photographer Helena Smith
Additional Photography Michelle Grant; John Heseltine; Paul Harris and Anne Heslope; James McConnachie; Roger Moss; Rough Guides: Helena Smith.
Fact Checker Cristina Dainotto

At DK INDIA
Managing Editor Aruna Ghose
Editorial Manager Sheeba Bhatnagar
Design Manager Kavita Saha
Project Editors Trisha Bora, Vatsala Srivastava
Project Designer Namrata Adhwaryu
Assistant Cartographic Manager Suresh Kumar
Cartographer Zafar-ul-Islam Khan
Maps
Lovell Johns Ltd
Base mapping supplied by Kartographie Huber, www.kartographie.de
Senior Picture Research Coordinator Taiyaba Khatoon
DTP Coordinator Azeem Siddiqui
DTP Designer Rakesh Pal
Indexer Andy Kulkarni
Proofreader George Theimi

At DK LONDON
Publisher Douglas Amrine
List Manager Julie Oughton
Design Manager Mabel Chan
Senior Editor Sadie Smith
Senior Cartographic Editor Casper Morris
Cartographer Stuart James
DTP Operator Jason Little
Production Controller Erika Pepe

Picture Credits
Placement Key- t=top; tc=top centre; tr=top right; cla=centre left above; ca=centre above; cra=centre right above; cl=centre left; c=centre; cr=centre right; clb=centre left below; cb=centre below; crb=centre right below; bl=bottom left; bc=bottom centre; br=bottom right; ftl=far top left; ftr=far top right; fcla=far centre left above; fcra=far centre right above; fcl=far centre left; fcr=far centre right; fclb=far centre left below; fcrb=far centre right below; fbl=far bottom left; fbr=far bottom right.

Every effort has been made to trace the copyright holders, and we apologize in advance for any unintentional omissions. We would be pleased to insert the appropriate acknowledgments in any subsequent edition of this publication.

Photography Permissions
Dorling Kindersley would like to thank the following for their assistance and kind permission to photograph at their establishments:

Antica Bottega del Vino, Verona; Antica Locanda dei Mercanti, Milan; Casa di Giulietta; Donizetti, Bergamo; Isola Bella; La Streccia, Cannobio; Mistrale Ristorante, Bellagio; Palazzo Te 1525, Mantova; Rocca Borromeo.

The publisher would like to thank the following individuals, companies, and picture libraries for their kind permission to reproduce their photographs:

4CORNERS IMAGES: SIME/ Johanna Huber 4-5.

ALAMY IMAGES: Krys Bailey 26-27c; CuboImages sr 36tc; Art Kowalsky 1c; MBP-Italia 6crb; Peter Mumford 18tr; Photo Ceolin 47tr; Visual&Written SL 58-9.

AMBROSIANA PICTURES: 36bl.

CAMPING NANZEL: 117tl.

CASCINA PIAN DI SPAGNA E BORGOFRANCONE : 116tl.

CORBIS: Grand Tour/ Sandra Raccanello/ 68-9; PoodlesRock 32bc.

CORSO COMO 10: Vanni Burkhart 52t.

PHOTO ARCHIVE ENIT: Sandro Bedessi 37tr, 37br; Gino Cianci 80tl; Andrea Lazzarini Editore 40tl.

FESTA DEL TORRONE: 37cl.

FESTIVAL DEL FILM LOCARNO: 36tr.

FONDAZIONE BERGAMO NELLA STORIA – MUSEO DONIZETTIANO: 78bc.

FRIENDLY RENTALS: 115tl.

PHOTOLIBRARY: 17bl, 32tc, 32tr, 33cl, 44tl, 44tc, 44tr; Michele Bella 41tr; Cash Cash 38tr; Gianalberto Cigolini 18bl; Doco Dalfiano 100-101; DEA/G Berengo Gardin 7clb; Brian Lawrence 40tr, 82-83; John Lawrence 30-31; LOOK-foto/ Andreas Strauss 39cl; Federico Meneghetti 21cra; Bruno Morandi 12-13c; Martin Moxter 46t; Siepmann Siepmann 57tl; Mark Edward Smith 45cl, 46bl; STOCK4B-RF STOCK4B-RF 40bl.

SETTIMANE MUSICALI DI STRESA E DEL LAGO MAGGIORE: 36tl.

VILLA D'ESTE: 52bl.

WIKIPEDIA, THE FREE ENCYCLOPEDIA: 32tl, 44bc, 73tl.

Front Flap: DK Images: Paul Harris and Anne Heslope fbr; Helena Smith tr, ftr, cra, bl, br. Cascina Pian di Spagna e Borgofrancone: fbl.

All other images © Dorling Kindersley
For further information see: www. dkimages.com

Special Editions of DK Travel Guides

DK Travel Guides can be purchased in bulk quantities at discounted prices for use in promotions or as premiums. We are also able to offer special editions and personalized jackets, corporate imprints, and excerpts from all of our books, tailored specifically to meet your own needs.

To find out more, please contact:

(in the United States) SpecialSales@ dk.com

(in the UK) travelspecialsales@ uk.dk.com

(in Canada) DK Special Sales at general@tourmaline.ca

(in Australia) business.development@ pearson.com.au

Phrase Book

In an Emergency

Help!	**Aiuto!**	eye-yoo-toh
Stop!	**Fermate!**	fair-mah-teh
Call a doctor.	**Chiama un medico**	kee-ah-mah oon meh-dee-koh
Call an ambulance.	**Chiama un' ambulanza**	kee-ah-mah oon am-boo-lan-tsa
Call the police.	**Chiama la polizia**	kee-ah-mah lah pol-ee-tsee-ah
Call the fire brigade.	**Chiama i pompieri**	kee-ah-mah ee pom-pee-air-ee

Communication Essentials

Yes/No	**Sì/No**	see/noh
Please	**Per favore**	pair fah-vor-eh
Thank you	**Grazie**	grah-tsee-eh
Excuse me	**Mi scusi**	mee skoo-zee
Hello	**Buon giorno**	bwon jor-noh
Goodbye	**Arrivederci**	ah-ree-veh-dair-chee
Good evening	**Buona sera**	bwon-ah sair-ah
What?	**Quale?**	kwah-leh?
When?	**Quando?**	kwan-doh?
Why?	**Perchè?**	pair-keh?
Where?	**Dove?**	doh-veh?

Useful Phrases

How are you?	**Come sta?**	koh-meh stah?
Very well, thank you.	**Molto bene, grazie.**	moll-toh beh-neh grah-tsee-eh
Pleased to meet you.	**Piacere di conoscerla.**	pee-ah-chair-eh dee-coh-noh-shair-lah
That's fine.	**Va bene.**	va beh-neh
Where is/are ...?	**Dov'è/ Dove sono ...?**	dov-eh/doveh soh-noh?
How do get to ...?	**Come faccio per arrivare a ...?**	koh-meh fah-choh pair arri-var-eh ah...?
Do you speak English?	**Parla inglese?**	par-lah een-gleh-zeh?
I don't understand.	**Non capisco.**	non ka-pee-skoh
I'm sorry.	**Mi dispiace.**	mee dee-spee-ah-cheh

Shopping

How much does this cost?	**Quant'è, per favore?**	kwan-the pair fah-vor-eh?
I would like ...	**Vorrei ...**	vor-ray
Do you have ...?	**Avete ...?**	ah-veh-teh ...?
Do you take credit cards?	**Accettate carte di credito?**	ah-chet-tah-the kar-teh dee creh-dee-toh?
What time do you open/close?	**A che ora apre/ chiude?**	ah keh or-ah ah-preh/kee-oo-deh?
this one	**questo**	kweh-stoh
that one	**quello**	kwell-oh
expensive	**caro**	kar-oh
cheap	**a buon prezzo**	ah bwon pret-soh
size, clothes	**la taglia**	lah tah-lee-ah
size, shoes	**il numero**	eel noo-mair-oh
white	**bianco**	bee-ang-koh
black	**nero**	neh-roh
red	**rosso**	ross-oh
yellow	**giallo**	jal-loh
green	**verde**	vair-deh
blue	**blu**	bloo

Types of Shop

bakery	**il forno /il panificio**	eel forn-oh /il /eel pan-ee-fee-choh
bank	**la banca**	lah bang-kah
bookshop	**la libreria**	lah lee-breh-ree-ah
cake shop	**la pasticceria**	lah pas-tee-chair-ee-ah
chemist	**la farmacia**	lah far-mah-chee-ah
delicatessen	**la salumeria**	lah sah-loo-meh-ree-ah
department store	**il grande magazzino**	eel gran-deh mag-gad-zee-noh
grocery	**alimentari**	ah-lee-men-tah-ree
hairdresser	**il parrucchiere**	eel par-oo-kee-air-eh
ice cream parlour	**la gelateria**	lah jel-lah-tair-ree-ah
market	**il mercato**	eel mair-kah-toh
newsstand	**l'edicola**	leh-dee-koh-lah
post office	**l'ufficio postale**	loo-fee-choh pos-tah-leh
supermarket	**il supermercato**	eel su-pair-mair-kah-toh
tobacconist	**il tabaccaio**	eel tah-bak-eye-oh
travel agency	**l'agenzia di viaggi**	lah-jen-tsee-ah dee vee-ad-jee

Sightseeing

art gallery	**la pinacoteca**	lah peena-koh-teh-kah
bus stop	**la fermata dell'autobus**	lah fair-mah-tah dell ow-toh-booss
church	**la chiesa basilica**	lah kee-eh-zah la lah bah-seel-i-kah
closed for holidays	**chiuso per le ferie**	kee-oo-zoh pair leh fair-ee-eh
garden	**il giardino**	eel jar-dee-no
museum	**il museo**	eel moo-zeh-oh
railway station	**la stazione**	lah stah-tsee-oh-neh
tourist information	**l'ufficio di turismo**	loo-fee-choh dee too-ree-smoh

Staying in a Hotel

Do you have any vacant rooms?	**Avete camere libere?**	ah-veh-teh kah-mair-eh lee-bair-eh?
double room	**una camera doppia**	oona kah-mair-ah doh-pee-ah
with double bed	**con letto matrimoniale**	kon let-toh-mah tree-moh-nee-ah-leh
twin room	**una camera con due letti**	oona kah-mair-ah kon doo-eh let-tee?
single room	**una camera singola**	oona kah-mair-ah sing-goh-lah
room with a bath, shower	**una camera con bagno, con doccia**	oona kah-mair-ah kon ban-yoh, kon dot-chah
I have a reservation.	**Ho fatto una prenotazione.**	oh fat-toh oona preh-noh-tah-tsee-oh-neh

126

Eating Out

Have you got a table for ...?	**Avete una tavola per ... ?**	ah-veh-teh oona tah-voh-lah pair ...?
I'd like to reserve a table	**Vorrei riservare una tavola.**	vor-ray ree-sair-vah-reh oona tah-voh-lah
breakfast	**colazione**	koh-lah-tsee-oh-neh
lunch	**pranzo**	pran-tsoh
dinner	**cena**	cheh-nah
The bill, please.	**Il conto, per favore.**	eel kon-toh pair fah-vor-eh
waitress	**cameriera**	kah-mair-ee-air-ah
waiter	**cameriere**	kah-mair-ee-aireh
fixed price menu	**il menù a prezzo fisso**	eel meh-noo ah pret-soh fee-soh
dish of the day	**piatto del giorno**	pee-ah-toh dell jor-no
starter	**antipasto**	an-tee-pass-toh
first course	**il primo**	eel pree-moh
main course	**il secondo**	eel seh-kon-doh
vegetables	**contorni**	eel kon-tor-noh
dessert	**il dolce**	eel doll-cheh
cover charge	**il coperto**	eel koh-pair-toh
wine list	**la lista dei vini**	lah lee-stah day vee-nee
glass	**il bicchiere**	eel bee-kee-air eh
bottle	**la bottiglia**	lah bot-teel-yah
knife	**il coltello**	eel kol-tell-oh
fork	**la forchetta**	lah for-ket-tah
spoon	**il cucchiaio**	eel koo-kee-eye-oh

Menu Decoder

l'acqua minerale gassata/ naturale	lah-kwah mee-nair-ah-leh gah-zah-tah/ nah-too-rah-leh	mineral water fizzy/still
agnello	ah-niell-oh	lamb
aglio	al-ee-oh	garlic
al forno	al for-noh	baked
alla griglia	ah-lah greel-yah	grilled
arrosto	ar-ross-toh	roast
la birra	lah beer-rah	beer
la bistecca	lah bee-stek-kah	steak
il burro	eel boor-oh	butter
il caffè	eel kah-feh	coffee
la carne	la kar-neh	meat
carne di maiale	kar-neh dee mah-yah-leh	pork
la cipolla	la chip-oh-lah	onion
i fagioli	ee fah-joh-lee	beans
il formaggio	eel for-mad-joh	cheese
le fragole	leh frah-goh-leh	strawberries
il fritto misto	eel free-toh mees-toh	mixed fried dish
la frutta	la froot-tah	fruit
frutti di mare	froo-tee dee mah-reh	seafood
i funghi	ee foon-ghee	mushrooms
i gamberi	ee gam-bair-ee	prawns
il gelato	eel jel-lah-toh	ice cream
l'insalata	leen-sah-lah-tah	salad
il latte	eel laht-teh	milk
lesso	less-oh	boiled
il manzo	eel man-tsoh	beef
l'olio	loh-lee-oh	oil
il pane	eel pah-neh	bread
le patate	leh pah-tah-teh	potatoes
le patatine fritte	leh pah-tah-teen-eh free-teh	chips
il pepe	eel peh-peh	pepper
il pesce	eel pesh-eh	fish
il pollo	eel poll-oh	chicken
il pomodoro	eel poh-moh-dor-oh	tomato
il prosciutto cotto/crudo	eel pro-shoo-toh kot-toh/kroo-doh	ham cooked/cured
il riso	eel ree-zoh	rice
il sale	eel sah-leh	salt
la salsiccia	lah sal-see-chah	sausage
succo d'arancia/ di limone	soo-koh dah-ran-chah/ dee lee-moh-neh	orange/lemon juice
il tè	eel teh	tea
la torta	lah tor-tah	cake/tart
l'uovo	loo-oh-voh	egg
vino bianco	vee-noh bee-ang-koh	white wine
vino rosso	vee-noh ross-oh	red wine
il vitello	eel vee-tell-oh	veal
le vongole	leh von-goh-leh	clams
lo zucchero	loh zoo-kair-oh	sugar
la zuppa	lah tsoo-pah	soup

Numbers

1	**uno**	oo nol|
2	**due**	doo-eh
3	**tre**	treh
4	**quattro**	kwat-roh
5	**cinque**	ching-kweh
6	**sei**	say-ee
7	**sette**	set-teh
8	**otto**	ot-toh
9	**nove**	noh-veh
10	**dieci**	dee-eh-chee
11	**undici**	oon-dee-chee
12	**dodici**	doh-dee-chee
13	**tredici**	tray-dee-chee
14	**quattordici**	kwat-tor-dee-chee
15	**quindici**	kwin-dee-chee
16	**sedici**	say-dee-chee
17	**diciassette**	dee-chah-set-the
18	**diciotto**	dee-chot-toh
19	**diciannove**	dee-chah-noh-veh
20	**venti**	ven-tee
30	**trenta**	tren-tah
40	**quaranta**	kwah-ran-tah
50	**cinquanta**	ching-kwan-tah
60	**sessanta**	sess-an-tah
70	**settanta**	set-tan-tah
80	**ottanta**	ot-tan-tah
90	**novanta**	noh-van-tah
100	**cento**	chen-toh
1,000	**mille**	mee-leh
2,000	**duemila**	doo-eh mee-lah
1,000,000	**un milione**	oon meel-yoh-neh

Time

one minute	**un minuto**	oon mee-noo-toh
one hour	**un'ora**	oon or-ah
a day	**un giorno**	oon jor-noh
Monday	**lunedì**	loo-neh-dee
Tuesday	**martedì**	mar-teh-dee
Wednesday	**mercoledì**	mair-koh-leh-dee
Thursday	**giovedì**	joh-veh-dee
Friday	**venerdì**	ven-air-dee
Saturday	**sabato**	sah-bah-toh
Sunday	**domenica**	doh-meh-nee-kah

Italian Lakes Town Index

Town	Ref	Town	Ref	Town	Ref
Abbazia di Piona	N2	Gardone Riviera	Q4	Pavia	C6
Albónico	P1	Gargnano	R3	Péglio	N1
Anfo	Q3	Garlate	P4	Peschiera del Garda	R5
Angera	J4	Garzeno	N2	Piacenza	D6
Arco	S1	Gavirate	K4	Pieve di Bono	R1
Argegno	M3	Gera Lário	P1	Pigra	M3
Arolo	K4	Germignaga	K3	Pino	K2
Arona	J4	Gerra	L2	Piodina	K2
Arsago	K5	Ghiffa	K3	Pisano	J4
Ascona	K1	Gordola	L1	Pisogne	F3
Assenza	S3	Gravedona	N1	Ponte Tresa	L3
Bagolino	Q2	Guello	N3	Ponti sul Mincio	R6
Bardolino	R5	Idro	Q3	Porlezza	M2
Baveno	J3	Intra	J3	Portese	Q4
Belgirate	J4	Iseo	E4	Porto	K3
Bellagio	N3	Isone	M2	Porto Ronco	K2
Bellano	N2	Ispra	K4	Porza	L2
Bellinzona	M1	Láglio	M3	Prada	R4
Bergamo	D3	Laorca	P3	Premeno	K3
Berzona	K1	Lardaro	R1	Progero	L1
Besozzo	K4	Laveno	K3	Pusiano	N4
Bezzecca	R2	Lazise	R5	Ranco	J4
Biandronno	K4	Lecco	P4	Rho	M6
Bidogno	M2	Legnano	L6	Riva del Garda	S2
Blévio	M4	Lenno	N3	Riva San Vitale	M3
Bogliaco	R4	Lesa	J4	Rivoltella	Q5
Bolognano	S2	Lézzeno	N3	Roveredo	M1
Bondone	Q2	Lido di Lonato	Q5	S. Bartolomeo	L1
Borgomanero	J5	Lierna	N3	S. Benedetto	R5
Brabbia	K4	Limone sul Garda	S2	S. Giovanni	S1
Brenzone	R3	Limonta	N3	S. Maria	N2
Brescia	F4	Locarno	L1	S. Zeno di Montagna	R4
Brienno	M3	Lodrone	Q2	Sala	L2
Brissago	K2	Lonato	Q5	Sala Comácina	N3
Brivio	P4	Lovere	F3	Salò	Q4
Brunate	M4	Lugaggia	M2	San Pellegrino Terme	D3
Busto Arsizio	L5	Lugano	L2	Saronno	M5
Cadenábbia	N3	Luino	K3	Sessa	L3
Cadenazzo	L1	Maccagno	K2	Seveso	M5
Calolziocorte	P4	Magadino	L1	Sirmione	R5
Calozzo Miánico	N2	Magliaso	L3	Sonvico	M2
Campione del Garda	R3	Magnago	L6	Stresa	J3
Campo	P1	Malcesine	S3	Taverne	L2
Cânnero	K2	Malesco	J2	Tenno	S2
Cannòbio	K2	Malgrate	P4	Ternate	K4
Capovalle	Q3	Mandello del Lário	N3	Tignale	R3
Carabietta	L3	Manerba d. Garda	Q5	Torbole	S2
Careno	N3	Mantova	H6	Tormini	Q4
Carlazzo	M2	Margno	P2	Torno	M4
Cavargna	M2	Masliánico	M4	Torri del Benaco	R4
Cavrasto	S1	Medéglia	M2	Tradate	L5
Cernóbbio	M4	Medolago	P5	Treménico	P2
Certosa di Pavia	C5	Meina	J4	Tremezzo	N3
Cima	M2	Melide	L3	Tremosine	R3
Cisano	R5	Menággio	N2	Treviso Bresciano	Q3
Civenna	N3	Mergozzo	J3	Turano	Q3
Claino Con Ósteno	M2	Mesenzana	K3	Val di Sogno	S3
Clusone	E3	Mezzolago	R2	Valbrona	N3
Colombare	R5	Miazzina	J3	Valvestino	Q3
Comabbio	K4	Milan	N6	Varedo	M5
Como	M4	Minusio	L1	Varenna	N2
Comologne	J1	Moltrásio	M4	Varese	L4
Corippo	L1	Moniga d. Garda	Q5	Varone	S2
Crémia	N2	Monvalle	K4	Verbania	J3
Cremona	E6	Monza	N6	Vercelli	A5
Cugnasco	L1	Morazzone	L4	Verona	H4
Darzo	Q2	Morcote	L3	Vesta	Q3
Desenzano	Q5	Nággio	N2	Vezia	L2
Dizzasco	M3	Nago	S2	Vigevano	B5
Domaso	N1	Navene	S3		
Dongo	N2	Nesso	N3		
Dório	N2	Nobiállo	N2		
Dumenza	L2	Novara	B4		
Erba	N4	Novate Mezzola	P1		
Gallarate	L5	Nuova Olónio	P1		
Gandria	M2	Oggebbio	K3		
Garda	R4	Onno	N3		
Gardaland	R5	Orta San Giulio	J4		
		Pacengo	R5		
		Pai	R4		
		Pallanza	J3		
		Paudo	M1		